GET OVER IT!

GET OVER IT!:
Relearning Guidance Practices

Daniel J. Hodgins

Copyright © 2013 by Daniel J Hodgins

All Rights Reserved. No part of this book may be reproduced, copied or utilized in any form or by any means, electronic, mechanical, photocopying, recording, or by any information storage and retrieval system, without permission in writing from the publisher. Inquiries should be addressed to: .
dkj5075@aol.com

Special thanks for photographs to:
   Heather Sordyl Pemble
   Amy Ahola, Child Central Station
   MCC Early Childhood Center

Manufactured in the United States of America

Thanks to the children who took me to the ***End Of My Rope.***

I am a better teacher because of you…

Contents

Helpful Charts • ix

Introduction
Should I really be a teacher? • xi

Part One:
Why Do Children Take Us To The End Of Our Rope? • 1

Chapter One:
Children Are Always Looking For What They're Good At • 3

Chapter Two:
How Do Adults Respond To Challenging Behaviors? • 9

Chapter Three:
What Are the Major Causes of Challenging Behaviors? • 13

Part Two:
Relearning Guidance Practices • 37

Chapter Four:
Making Sure the Curriculum is Relevant • 39

Chapter Five:
Environments That Support Children • 49

Chapter Six:
Share Soothing Skills • 55

Chapter Seven:
Focus On What You Want Them To Do • 61

Chapter Eight:
Helping Children Express Anger • 65

Chapter Nine:
They Are Not The Terrible Twos; They Are Just Toddlers • 71

CHAPTER TEN:
Avoid Emphasis On Sharing • 75

CHAPTER ELEVEN:
Avoid Mislabeling Highly Active and Highly Bored Children, Attention Deficient Hyperactive Disorder (ADHD) • 79

CHAPTER TWELVE:
Developing a Climate of Respect • 83

CHAPTER THIRTEEN:
Avoid Chaotic Transition Times • 87

CHAPTER FOURTEEN:
Use Encouragement Statements Rather than Praise • 93

CHAPTER FIFTEEN:
Providing "Real" Choices • 97

CHAPTER SIXTEEN:
Support Risk Taking • 101

CHAPTER SEVENTEEN:
Fighting? • 105

CHAPTER EIGHTEEN:
Preventing Power Struggles • 109

CHAPTER NINETEEN:
Bring Back Roughhousing • 113

CHAPTER TWENTY:
Supporting Super Hero Play • 117

CHAPTER TWENTY-ONE:
Creating a Place to Belong • 121

CONCLUSION:
Do I Really Have to Change? • 125

ADDITIONAL RESOURCES • 127

Helpful Charts

Relearning Guidance Practices • xiii

What Are Some Actions Children Are Good At? • 5

Guidance: Redirecting or Reinventing • 7

The Hardest Part of Being a Good Teacher • 11

Changing Unclear Messages • 17

New Rules for Early Childhood Settings • 21

Setting Up Guardrails • 22

Tips that Lead to Successful Experiences for Children • 26

Strategies for Keeping Behaviors of Young Children at Their Developmental Level • 28

Common Unmet Needs • 34

Relearning Guidance Strategies • 35

How to Make a Relevant Curriculum • 42

Elements in Supportive Environments • 50, 51

Developing Supportive Environments • 53

Focusing on Positive Statements • 63

Common Causes of Anger in Children • 66

Anger Releases • 67

Children's Books • 69

What Do Toddlers Need? • 73

Toddler Spaces • 74

Helpful Hints For Not Sharing • 76

Activities that Support the Active Child • 81

Establishing a Climate of Respect • 84

Clean Up Tips • 90

Encouragement Statements • 96

Risk Taking Possibilities • 103

Relearning Guidance Practices for Fighting • 107

Power Builders • 111

Activities that Support Roughhousing • 115

What is Needed to Create that Environment of "Belonging" • 123

Introduction:
Should I really be a teacher?

When I first started teaching, thirty plus years ago, I began to wonder if I really should be a teacher. Lots of teachers around me were saying, "I became a teacher because I love all kids!" and I didn't. What I found out was they really didn't mean all children, but only children that did what they requested. When they said, "Children, in five more minutes it will be time to pick up," those children who did pick up, they loved. When a child came up to them and requested a Kleenex in case their nose dripped, they really loved. The children who did not pick up or used the teacher's pant leg or shirtsleeve for a Kleenex, they did not love. These teachers also treated children differently based on whether or not they followed through with the request.

I knew quickly that I wanted to be a teacher. One that didn't necessarily have to love all children, but a teacher that accepted and celebrated all children's differences. Yes, even those that wiped their noses on me.

Some children spend much of their time creating situations that might take us to the End of Our Rope. Adults often treat these creative and adventurous children differently. Have you ever said to yourself, when the child who creates challenges doesn't show up, "There is a God"? Have you ever wished a mild case of "chickenpox" on that child, to keep him/her out for a couple of weeks? It sometimes seems like that child is never absent.

So many guidance challenges that occur in early childhood programs are not the fault of children but often are caused by curriculum and environmental practices developed by adults.

There are three questions that early childhood professionals should ask themselves when developing guidance techniques:

- What do I believe about children?
- What practices do I use that reflect what I believe about children?
- What do I have to change to make sure my beliefs and practices match?

Many times beliefs about children are not reflected in practices. This creates challenges for children and adults. For example, we know children are egocentric but often I hear, "We share our toys in school." The belief in this case, children have difficulty sharing, doesn't fit the practice of asking children to share.

To help make practices fit what we know and believe about children, we must dare to relearn techniques. We must search through our lifetime of experiences, knowledge and observations to stimulate a different creation of guidance practices that support all children.

This book is divided into two sections. Part I details the major causes of challenging behaviors, including but not limited to unclear messages, too many rules, creating failure opportunities, learning styles, testing limits and difficult lives. Part II provides insight into practical strategies that are proven effective with children who take us to the end of our rope. Included are setting up environments of support, creating power building opportunities, supporting unmet needs, providing "real choices" and developing a climate of trust.

Relearning guidance practices is not a simple task. There is no step-by-step method that fits all situations for all children.

The following pages are filled with practical suggestions that have been put to test in many early childhood environments that I've visited. You will not find one solution that meets all situations, instead you will gain new insights that will excite, motivate and cause you to relearn. This will transform your setting into a place that children want to be in.

Introduction: Should I Really be a Teacher? xiii

RELEARNING GUIDANCE PRACTICES

Fill in the empty spaces

Beliefs	Practices	Changes
1. Children can't share	Multiples of toys	No time limits
2. Children are active	Providing for running, jumping, climbing	Create a safe environment
3.		
4.		
5.		
6.		
7.		
8.		
9.		
10.		

PART I

Why Do Children Take Us To The End Of Our Rope?

1 Children Are Always Looking For What They're Good At

I'm Good At Pushing…

Children with challenging behaviors are often looking for what they are good at. Adults often give attention to negative behaviors that challenging children are good at.

Here's a chant I like to do with children (When they say the word push, they get to push the person next to them):

Chris Is His Name

Chris is his name
And pushing is his game.
You can catch him pushing
In the sun and rain.
He is pushing high,
And pushing low.
He is pushing, pushing
Wherever he goes.
So if you want some pushing
And you don't know what to do
Just go ask Chris
And he'll help you.

The important question here is, What is Chris Good At? The answer of course is PUSHING. He is not bad at pushing; he is very good at it.

Every human being responds to acknowledgement, which reinforces caring, appreciation and respect. Children that are constantly criticized begin feeling that they may as well give up trying and they have no hope of achieving success. Some children who feel unworthy set out to prove themselves to the world. This may include many behaviors that are often not accepted in early childhood settings. Misbehavior increases when children are not permitted to show what they are good at.

Jacob was a "hitter." Whenever any child would come close to him, he would hit them or push them down.

The children often would cry and the teacher would come over and say, "We don't hit in our school!" The problem is that Jacob has been hitting in school and he is pretty good at it. It is crucial that we provide something for Jacob to "HIT" and recognize what he is good at by saying, "You really like to hit. Hit this box as hard as you can."

We need to step back and rethink what children can and cannot do based on their stage of development. Children are not "bad" because they push, take, or leave activities not interesting to them. They are displaying behaviors that fit their growth and development.

A preschool program invited me to observe a child in their setting. The staff viewed the child as displaying some behaviors that were disruptive. During my observation I saw this child push another child who came to close to a tower he was building, grab a truck that another child was playing with, and during story reading stood up and walked away only to be brought back twice by a staff member. After observing the child for the morning session the staff seemed to be very excited to sit with me to discuss strategies that might be used to change his behaviors. What surprised them was my response. I didn't see anything the child did that was not typical for that age. Not only was it typical for his stage of development, but also everything the child did, he was "Good At" doing.

Perhaps the problem is that we have forgotten what children are good at. Have you ever heard a child swear? They usually don't swear poorly. They are pretty good at it, swearing in complete sentences, clear and precise.

WHAT ARE SOME ACTIONS CHILDREN ARE GOOD AT?

- Taking what they see and like
- Keeping it until they are done with it
- Taking it home if they really like it
- Pushing to get it
- Letting everyone know it belongs to them
- Giving it to someone when they are done with it

It is important, when working with young children, that we keep in mind what they can and what they are unable to do yet:

- **Children don't share well** – they are egocentric and believe that everything that is provided in our program belongs to them and only them
- **Children frequently don't recognize that someone else has the same needs and wishes they have** – they often take objects that another child is playing with because they think that child wants them to have it
- **Children only remember what is relevant to them** – if it is not relevant it will be forgotten (Walk, Listen, Stop)
- **Children can't sit for very long** – a preschooler's body is crying out for movement; sitting is unnatural
- **Children have a hard time expressing themselves using words** – they often use physical means of communication (Pushing, Shoving, Hitting)
- **Children have a difficult time understanding the differences between right and wrong** – they often don't relate to cause and effect relationships

Lots of information is being distributed lately regarding Bullies. Bullies are not born that way; they become bullies because they get lots of status for being one. They are essentially good at being a Bully. A Bully believes, "If I can't be the best, I'll be the worst!" So he/she becomes really good at being the "worst." The really sad part is that victims become really good at being "victims." Remember you don't have bullies unless you have victims. So the attention should be placed on the victims, not the bullies. We must help victims become good at not being victims. Victims often become good at whining, crying, or worse yet, taking it. We must help them become good at saying, "No!" "Keep your hands away from me!" and "I need help solving this."

Encouragement says you value them, without comparison to others. It bestows motivation, it renews energy, it gives children the courage to continue difficult tasks and develops independence to reach out for new levels of achievement.

In giving encouragement, you can help children set realistic goals for themselves based on their individual capacities and personalities. Such learning will keep them from giving up when things seem to be getting more difficult. They will gradually build their skills in accordance with their growing capabilities, acquiring self-respect and strength at what they are good at.

> *You don't have bullies unless you have victims*

Whenever I am involved with a child who takes me to the end of my rope, I use the following guidance format.

Put the child's name on the top of the paper and list all the things he or she is good at. Then, focus on supporting those behaviors by redirection or reinventing different practices.

GUIDANCE: REDIRECTING OR REINVENTING

Name of Child _____

Behaviors the child is good at	Practices to Support
1. Hitting	Boxes for hitting
2. Burping	Ignore
3.	
4.	
5.	
6.	
7.	
8.	

Get Over It!: Relearning Guidance Practices

How Do Adults Respond To Challenging Behaviors?

"I think he wakes up in the morning planning to drive me nuts!"

When faced with challenging behaviors of children, adults often respond differently depending on their belief about the causes.

The following are the typical responses:

- *Perceive the behavior as deliberate noncompliance* – this is the adult who says, "Jack hits because he is a 'mean' one" or "I think Susan wakes up in the morning with an attitude."

- *Attempt to control* – this is the adult who says, "If you continue hitting, you will have to stay in when we go outside" or "Listen when I talk to you."

- *Neglect to address the needs of the child* – this is the adult who says, "Sit in the time out chair and think about why you hit him," or "You have to share with your friends at school."

- *Engage in Power Struggles* – this is the adult who says, "I am not going to tell you again" or "If you don't pick up, you won't get to play with them again."

These types of responses directly affect the children's behaviors. Children learn at a very early age to mistrust adults. By the time they are two years of age, many children have been tricked, coerced and cheated by adults. They develop a feeling that it is safer not to trust than to be fooled again and again.

The misbehavior of some children is seldom what it first appears to be. Understanding this is the only place to start. No child has a need to create a life of conflict.

Children that adults have come to dislike are the most challenging.

Arick was the child in my teaching experience that changed my practices for the rest of my life. For the first three weeks of school, this child came in every morning yelling, "Good morning STUPID DAN." To me, a highly educated person, it didn't take long to realize Arick was asking for acknowledgement.

At first I responded with, "Don't call me stupid, that isn't nice."

Arick would then respond with, "Stupid, Stupid, Stupid."

I changed my approach to, "I have been waiting for you, Arick, and by the way you have part of my name right, Dan." I wanted Arick to know what part of his statement was right and by giving him acknowledgement the name-calling stopped.

Emotionally driven children are distinguished by their ability to elicit from others exactly the opposite of what they really need.

It takes courage to give real trust. We're so used to controlling children by *ifs* ("If you don't do that now, you won't get to play with this again") that it is a complete turnabout to place faith in them. Children need to be able to trust us to empathize with them when they are crying but not probe and compound the issues by making them recount what happened. Yet they know that you are ready to listen, nonjudgmentally, when they want to tell you what happened or why they are crying. They need to be able to trust you to allow them to fail and to give them encouragement when they want to try again. They need to be able to trust us not to have expectations of them that are so high that they can't live up to them and to know that we don't expect them to be perfect.

A trusting environment for children needs to be one that allows risk-taking, provides open, honest and caring relationships and includes a place for them to belong.

So many of us remember those teachers in our lives that demeaned, belittled or degraded our sense of self. In most cases their actions were unconscious—thinking they were doing the right thing. We can use those examples to prevent us from becoming what we didn't want.

Bev Bos, teacher, author, and friend says, "You should be the teacher you always wanted, not the teacher you want to be."

THE HARDEST PART OF BEING A GOOD TEACHER

Teachers report, "The hardest part of being a good teacher" is:

- Keeping my cool
- Finding time individually for each child
- Following through on things I expect
- Having patience
- Knowing the best way to model values and behavior
- Being consistent with practices
- Restraining my anger
- Not expecting more than children can give
- Avoiding power struggles
- Not taking what children say personally
- Addressing the needs of children
- Not getting "hooked" by the children

12 GET OVER IT!: RELEARNING GUIDANCE PRACTICES

 What Are the Major Causes of Challenging Behaviors?

"It's not my fault"

When we try to understand what causes major behavioral challenges with children, we need to go beyond their behavior to factors they have no control of. Particularly when the children continuously are involved in the same behaviors. Great care should be taken to look for possible underlying causes. The adults in their lives create many of the causes, not the children. This is difficult for us to look at because it requires that *we* change, not the child.

Some of the major causes of behavior challenges are explored in this chapter. You may find one or more related to the children you are working with.

UNCLEAR MESSAGES—SAYING WHAT WE MEAN

Clarifying messages is an important method for discipline. Not only does it mean good communication, but also it can prevent misunderstandings. Clarification means that when you request things from children, you do so in clear, precise terms that leave no room for misunderstanding. How many times have you given a direction or made a comment, to an adult, that you thought was perfectly clear only to find out that the receiver of the comment heard something totally different than you expected. "Will you start the washing and I will finish it when I get home?" You were expecting that the person who received this request would put the clothes in the washing machine to start the process and you would finish it when you return. Instead the receiver sorts the clothes and leaves them on the floor for you to do.

In making requests and comments to children, be sure that the children understand what you are asking. Consider their individual abilities and development. Don't expect a three year old to respond with the same understanding of a five year old. Keep the words as simple as possible. State exactly what you want children to do avoiding lengthy rationale.

If the message is unclear to children, they will interpret it anyway they wish. The interpretation may be completely different than the message sent.

Here are some examples of the most common unclear messages I often hear:

"Use your inside voice" – what the heck is an inside voice? Children come to us from many homes where the "inside voice" is screaming as loud as you can to get heard. Derrick was playing in the block area and started to yell, "Watch out—the fire is spreading!" He was pretending there was a fire burning his structure. The teacher went over and said, "Derrick, use your inside voice." He put his hands up to his mouth and started to scream, "Fire, Fire, Fire." Derrick thought that if he covered his mouth with his hands that would be his inside voice. If we believe that all children are different, than we must accept that many children have different "inside voices." Is one better than the other? I don't think so…

Do we give children the message that "quiet" is better than "loud"?

At a circle time, Sara was sitting waiting for the teacher to read a story. Some boys next to her were laughing. The teacher began to sing this song, "I like the way Sara's listening. I like the way Sara's listening. I like the way that Sara's listening. Let's all listen like Sara." Sara smiled and the boys looked at her and continued their laughter. The message the teacher was giving was that Sara is better than the boys. I worry that all Sara has learned is how to be compliant.

"Use your walking feet" – children think they are walking when they are running. Their brain says to their bodies, especially boys, run a lot here. Testosterone spikes in preschool aged boys can occur often throughout the day. During these spikes running occurs frequently. As early childhood professionals we need to respond by providing more spaces for running, both indoors and outdoors. Walking is not a natural action for children. It requires a conscious effort to walk.

Hallways invite children to run. Where did we come up with the rule, "No running in the hallway"? Let's change that to, "Make sure you run in the hallway!"

If children are encouraged to walk rather than run, we take the risk of them not developing confidence in their bodies.

Charley was a preschool age child in my classroom who would run from one end of the room to another, pushing a chair. This behavior repeated itself throughout the day. He would run so fast that he would knock children over that were in his way. He didn't see them, because running was his goal. The children soon figured out that running with this chair was something that Charley liked to do. So when they saw him coming, they yelled, "He's coming, move out of his way!" and they would all scatter. When he moved a little too fast, I just sat in his chair that he was pushing, to slow him down.

"Be nice to your friends" – there are two words here that are unclear—"Nice" and "Friends." If you were in a room full of adults and you asked them what they thought the word "nice" meant, you would probably get many different definitions. It is a very abstract word that often relates to actions rather than feelings. Some children think they are really "nice" when they take a toy away from another child, because they think that child wants them to have it. Carolyn pushed Jamie off a chair at the snack table and the teacher said, "That isn't a very nice thing to do to Jamie." Carolyn looked up at the teacher and said, "But it is my chair and she wasn't very nice sitting in it."

"Friends" is even more abstract and unclear. Most young children do not have friends; they have intruders. Children are so egocentric in their thought process that it is difficult to perceive a child as a friend who is taking his/or her blocks.

I have heard early childhood professionals say to a child who had hit another child, "We don't hit our friends." Since young children don't have friends, that statement gives him/her permission to hit most of the children in the classroom.

I avoid any statements that include the word "friends" when making requests or comments to young children. For example, "Friends, it is almost time to pick up," "Friends, it is time to get ready to go outside," and the worse, "Look at all our friends' smiling faces." Some children look at each other during these statements wondering whom the teacher is talking to.

"Use kinder words" – just what is a kinder word? Arick went up to Jessica and called her "poopy butt." The teacher said to him, "That is not a very kind thing to say to Jessica."

Arick got real close to Jessica and whispered, "You poopy butt." He thought that saying it softer was kinder.

When working with children who take you to the end of your rope, their response to your words is less important than the seeds of thought you plant while talking to them. Words trigger misbehavior as readily as actions.

Children who call other children names do not view it as an unkind action, but an action of power. It gets an immediate response from the child who is being called the name and any adult who is within hearing distance. A nine-year-old boy called me "Butt head." He expected me immediately to respond with, "Don't you ever call me that name." Instead my response was, "Are you talking to my head or my butt? Because my head is the only part of my body that is listening."

"In five more minutes, it will be time to clean up" – this is the most common unclear message that I hear everywhere. The first part of the message, "In five more minutes," is very unclear because young children do not have any concept of time. Time is the last cognitive concept for most children to grasp and many times it doesn't occur until after nine years of age. You might even know some adults who still haven't grasped the concept. Young children sing, "Jingle Bells" all year around or they say, "Tomorrow is my birthday," and it really isn't happening until two months away. The second part, "Time to clean up" is unclear because most adults expect that children will clean up everything they played with and children might not see that task as part of the play experience. Children's brains are asking, "Clean up what?", "How Much?", "Why would you want me to put this away?" Many early childhood professionals have asked me, "If we don't have children pick up, won't they be 'slops' as they get older?" There is no evidence to prove this. Clean up is not the most important concept for children to grasp. Some children enjoyed cleaning up—let them.

My daughter's definition of mess is, "You leave things out, so you know what you have." It doesn't mean that she doesn't clean up, it just isn't that important in the terms of priority of world events.

Here are some examples of unclear messages and how to change them to clear messages and/or actions:

CHANGING UNCLEAR MESSAGES	
Unclear Message	**Clear Message/Action**
"Get ready so we can go outside"	"Put on your coat so we can go outside"
"Those books don't belong on the floor"	"Put the books on this shelf"
"Use your walking feet"	"Run over here"
"That's not nice to push"	"It is fun to push, let me find something for you to push"
"Use your inside voice"	"Let me find a place you can use that voice"
"In five more minutes it will be time to clean up"	"Let me know when you are finished and I will help you put them back"

Too Many Rules

Have you ever went on a drive in the mountains and noticed the metal guardrails that are provided along the edge of the roads? They are there to keep us on the path. Notice how often they are scratched, marked and dented up. Some drivers, when they look to the left or right, move the steering wheel in that direction. The guardrails prevent them from going over the edge. Rules should be set up as "Guardrails," setting up the environment so that children are guided, given choices and helped from going over the edge.

Guardrails:
- Must be simple (clear and precise), not more than five words
- Must have consistent follow through (never have a rule that you won't follow through with)
- Must pertain to the child's stage of understanding (different guidelines for different stages of understanding)
- Must be enforceable (don't have a rule that you cannot enforce)
- Must be individual, not group (when we have group rules, egocentric children believe you are not talking to them)
- Must provide some choices (helps the child develop self-control)
- Must be limited (relate to health and safety only)

When setting guardrails they should be founded logically on concerns for health and safety. The child's ability to use logic doesn't really begin to develop until the elementary school years, and even then it takes time for children to become skilled in its use.

Charles Hughes (1991) said for children to be able to follow rules the following skills are needed:
- Skill 1 – sensitivity to the viewpoints of others
- Skill 2 – ability for mutual understanding
- Skill 3 – willingness to delay gratification
- Skill 4 – high degree of cooperation

Doesn't sound like many preschoolers I have observed. Matter of fact, I know some adults who do not have these skills fully developed yet.

What a child is looking for in a guardrail is not what they can't do, but what they can do. Most rules are set up to support the negative rather than the positive.

Rules that are often broken:

- "No running"
- "No hitting"
- "No taking toys from someone else"
- "No loud voices"

All of these rules state what the child cannot do. In most cases the expectations are too high for young children. For example, do we really expect children never to "HIT"?

Some adults set rules based on the rules they had as children themselves. It is like they are under the "spell," perhaps from their family rules, their neighborhood rules, their school rules or their religious rules.

Think about the rules you had from your childhood

Do you remember any of the following?

- *"No elbows on the table"* – Why? Will they fall off?
- *"Eat everything off your plate, there are people starving in China"* – Did you ever want to ship your vegetables to those starving people?
- *"Were you born in a barn?"* – I don't remember
- *"What happens in this house, stays in this house"* – No one is interested anyhow
- *"Always wear clean underwear when you go out of the house, because you never know when you are going to get in an accident"* – this is why most people have clean underwear on today when they leave their house

Many people still have these rules whether they make sense or not. I still look to see if my mother is watching me when I place my elbows on the table and she has been dead for many years now.

Children cannot distinguish between right and wrong until their frontal lobe has fully developed. Some researchers are indicating that frontal lobe development for girls is between 16 and 18 years of age. For boys it is even later, between the ages of 19 and 21 years.

HERE ARE SOME EXAMPLES OF FRONTAL LOBE STATEMENTS:

- *"Make a better choice"*
- *"How would you like it if someone hit you?"*
- *"You don't want to hurt your friends do you?"*
- *"Use your words, not your hands"*

If you have children that take you to the end of your rope, they often are looking for power. Sometimes they attain power by breaking rules you cannot enforce. For example, "Go to sleep right now!" Or "Eat everything off your plate, if you want to go out!" How do you enforce these rules legally? As soon as children realize they can attain power by breaking your rules, the race is on to see how often that can happen. Negative rules (Don't talk so loud, don't chew gum) set an adversarial tone in your setting, and serve as a constant reminder of the fastest way to obtain attention.

NEW RULES FOR EARLY CHILDHOOD SETTINGS

- Run a lot here

- Climb high

- Be loud

- Dig to China

- Hit this box

- Build higher than your eyes

- Avoid sharing

- Only listen when it is relevant

- Look at it before you flush it!

The following is a brief checklist for setting up guardrails in your environment:

SETTING UP GUARDRAILS

- ✓ Be precise
- ✓ Be consistent
- ✓ Say something only once
- ✓ Don't argue
- ✓ Remain flexible
- ✓ Give choices
- ✓ Keep it simple
- ✓ State what you want to happen
- ✓ Only should relate to health and safety issues
- ✓ Overlook small annoyances
- ✓ Get Over It!

FEELINGS OF FAILURE

Adults who work with children don't wake up in the morning saying, "I plan on causing failure today!" Unconsciously there are environmental and curriculum experiences that are developed that sometimes cause feelings of failure.

FOLLOWING ARE SOME EXAMPLES:

- *Competition* – "Let's see who can pick up the fastest." What if I am slow at it, or decide it is not what I want to be good at. Does this give the message that children who are not "fast at picking up" are failures at it?

- *Standing in line* – Invites children to push the child in front of them. When they push and get in trouble they often are punished for something they did not cause.

- *Waiting my turn* – This is a skill that is very difficult for young children. The longer the waiting time, the more challenging behaviors occur. John was standing near the easel, waiting to paint, when he said to Juliet, "Stop painting so much, my hands what to paint."

- *Asking children to share* – Young children don't recognize that other children have the same needs as they have. I worry more about children who do not take items from other children than children who do.

- *Expecting them to act like a little adult* – Asking children to adjust to behaviors that are more "adult like" causes lots of feeling of failure when they cannot live up to the expectations.

Most mental health specialists agree that a healthy attachment with a primary caregiver appears to be associated with a high probability of healthy relationships. Without predictable, responsive, nurturing and sensory-enriched caregiving, a child's potential for normal bonding and attachment will not be realized.

Our brain's "wiring" for healthy relationships depend on having the right kind of experiences of success at the right points of life.

Early childhood professionals are now playing a key role in attachment and bonding.

A larger percent of children are placed in programs outside of the home. Therefore, we cannot take the risk of "screwing up!"

The fit between adults and the children that will be arriving at their door is crucial.

> YOU CAN DO SEVERAL THINGS TO PROMOTE SUCCESS RATHER THAN FAILURE:
>
> - *Provide consistency in caregivers.* This is essential, especially for boys. Children's brains struggle with changes in the team of adults who care for them. Behavioral challenges increase when the consistency of staff changes frequently.
>
> - *Provide consistency in activities.* Children need a stable daily routine. Avoid major changes in their schedule. Young children thrive with ordered routine. When children know what to expect, they make choices that promote learning. Mr. Rogers always started his show by entering the door, taking off his outside shoes and blazer, replacing them with tennis shoes and a more casual sweater. These actions said to the viewers: We are starting the program now. Young children thrive for ordered routines such as this one.
>
> - *Offer regular opportunities for appropriate physical connection.* The more the body has a chance to move, the more connections that take place in the brain.
>
> - *Keep staff-child ratio high and class size low.* Children need enough caregivers to go around. Children have more difficulty adapting and changing when stress is present in the classroom.
>
> - *Support all children.* Children need to be aware when they arrive at your door you will be supporting their different needs. The active child, the loud child, the quiet child all need to know that, "You have been waiting for them!" and do not plan on changing who they are.

L. Tobin wrote something that I constantly think about when I am working with children who take me to the end of my rope.

"When a child is placed in failure experiences he/she will do anything to avoid it. Even if that means getting hurt or hurting. Failure adds so much stress to the brain." This statement guides me when I develop support strategies for children. It reminds me to look at the experiences a child is having and make sure that failure opportunities are removed. If a child is afraid of failure, he/she may say, "I can't," and avoid trying. If a child becomes discouraged by failure, he/she may say, "I won't," and refuse to try.

OBSERVE CHILDREN WHO SAY THE FOLLOWING OFTEN:

- "I can't"
- "I'm no good at painting"
- "I'm a jerk"
- "Nobody likes me"
- "I never get to win"
- "Shut up stupid"
- "I hate all of you"

These negative statements might reflect a child who is feeling like a failure. It is easier for a child who is feeling like a failure to use negative thinking. Make sure that you are not the person creating these feelings…

TIPS THAT LEAD TO SUCCESSFUL EXPERIENCES FOR CHILDREN:

- *Call children by their names* ("honey" only comes in a bottle or jar)
- *Learn about their world* (specifically about what they like and don't like)
- *Avoid making judgments* ("quiet" does not necessarily mean "better")
- *Touch in subtle ways* ("high fives," back rubs, hand shakes)
- *Encourage children to move often* (stretching, rolling, climbing)
- *Smile*, remembering that this provides immediate, positive feedback
- *Let the children decorate their own walls* This says to children, "Come on in, this is your place"
- *Make sure the environment supports their needs* Get down on your knees in the classroom and make sure what you see is what the children want to see
- *Have fun with children* If you are not having fun this job is not for you

DEVELOPMENTAL ISSUES VS. MORAL ISSUES

Derrick was sitting in the classroom picking his nose, not bothering anyone. The teacher came up to him and said, "Derrick it isn't nice to pick your nose. You might get germs and people won't like you if you pick your nose."

This is an example of an adult who turned a normal developmental issue into a moral issue.

Talking about the behavior as "not nice" and "people won't like you" takes a moral stand that often young children do not have the cognitive abilities to understand. Keeping this situation at a developmental level is best by simply handing the child a Kleenex and saying, "Store that in here!" It is interesting to me that if someone gets something in their eye they are supported in removing it. If there is something in the nose and someone tries to remove it that behavior is considered "not nice."

These are the most typical developmental behaviors of young children that seem to bother adults most frequently:

- *Picking their nose*
- *Pushing/Shoving another child*
- *Not listening to an adult*
- *Taking toys from other children*

Most of these developmental behaviors are responded to with statements like, "That isn't nice," "That is not a very friendly thing to do," "That is rude" or "People won't like you if you continue with that kind of behavior." All of these statements have some moral implication. It is important that we keep the strategy that we use with children at their developmental level. Avoid a strategy that uses a moral implication. Children's brains are not set up to receive those messages yet.

Keep strategies at a developmental level!

STRATEGIES FOR KEEPING BEHAVIORS OF YOUNG CHILDREN AT THEIR DEVELOPMENTAL LEVEL	
Behavior	**Strategy**
Picking their nose	Hand them a Kleenex
Pushing/Shoving	Push this box
Not listening	Change what you are saying
Taking toys	Provide multiples of toys
Name-calling	Give the child's name
Swearing	Give an acceptable word

When young children have to choose between being "nice" or being "bad" they are more likely to choose "bad" because it is simply easier to live up to.

At a workshop I was presenting, a mother of a young child asked, "How do you get a five-year-old to make a bed?"

My answer was, "Buy him a sleeping bag."

It wasn't the answer she was expecting.

The child would go into the bedroom and try to make the bed.

The mother would come in and say, "You call that made?"

Would you want to continue to make the bed if someone came in and scolded you for not making it to their expectation? This mother thought that making the bed was a sign of a "good child." If she wanted the bed made, keeping it at the developmental level of the child, a sleeping bag could be smoothed out and the child and adult would feel accomplished.

When I am presenting I often ask the audience, "Who are the people who can't leave their house without their bed made?" Those people who raise their hands are asked to explain why. Most of their responses are related to, "It makes me feel better," "I like the bed clean and organized when I get back into it," or "This is what my mother taught me."

Then I ask the audience, "Who are the people who do not make their beds?" Again those people who raise their hands were asked to explain why.

Most of their responses are related to, "Why make it when I am going to get back into it anyhow?" "It seems to be a waste of time," or "I used to have to make my bed all the time and now I don't want to."

Which behaviors are "better" or "nice"? They both are. Yet the 'bed-makers' and the 'non bed-makers' feel strongly that their behaviors are the best.

We need to examine the effects of any guidance approach we use as well as our motives for using it. If our real motive is to demonstrate authority, superiority and power, then the guidance approach for its own sake is more important than the children being guided.

If we believe that children can achieve growth only through a strict system that supports moral implications, than guidance is merely a system for filling our children's minds with data and fear. We have to ask ourselves what children ultimately will learn from our use of guidance strategies. Will they learn that children should be seen and not heard, follow but not lead, be informed but not to think?

Adults need to be sure that we use humane methods of guidance practices that support developmental levels of children. Our aim should be to convey such basic human values as respect, trust, honesty, and caring for others.

Wanting Attention—You can never get enough of it

Young children get lots of attention when they:

- *Scream*
- *Run away from you*
- *Hit*
- *Throw a tantrum*
- *Smile when they have done something you don't like*
- *Say, "Make me, you're not my mother!"*
- *Make enemies*
- *Make "all hell break loose"*

In struggling to develop independence, in wanting greater control of their own lives, children encounter great frustration. Their ways of expressing that frustration are often irritating to adults.

For example, some children acquire the habit of tattling when their own self-esteem has been impacted, when their own misbehaviors have been pointed out over and over again and when they have not been given attention for acceptable behaviors.

Whining is another habit that seems to be one of the most irritating to professionals. Children are not born whining. Often it develops from hearing adults speak in that special tone of voice, raised higher than the normal speaking level.

How many times have you heard adults whine? Example: "All it has been doing lately is raining. Isn't it ever going to stop?"

"We never go anywhere. Can't we take a little vacation?"

"When are we going to get paid for what we are worth?"

In a preschool classroom I observed, Julie was a perfect whiner.

Whenever an adult went up to her she would practice with them.

Julie would say during clean up time, "I don't know how to pick up these blocks, they are too heavy," or at the snack table, "I don't know how to pour my juice, it might spill" or at outside time, "I never get to ride the bike, no one likes me." Adults always gave her attention by rescuing her rather than helping her figure out the solutions for herself.

Temper tantrums, like so many other undesirable behaviors, are often an emotional reaction to not being able to control. They are a powerful attention-getting device. When temper tantrums are eliminated the attention they get is eliminated. When children throw tantrums they have an audience. Children go through developmental stages in which testing the limits of their own control is very important. A constant theme in children who take us to the end of our rope is to feel in control of their lives as much as possible. Testing limits is one of the ways children try out that control. They watch to see if you approve—and how far they can go if you disapprove. This helps them build their feelings of autonomy and independence. Sometimes children will deliberately try to do something they know you disapprove of to test whether you really care.

When I was teaching cooperative nursery school, Arick, four years of age, decided to test my limits. We were having ten ministers visit our classroom to see whether they wanted to donate $10,000 for our playground development. Our classroom was on its best behavior. The room smelled like lemons, we served pineapple and other fresh fruit for snack (which was a luxury), and we had many parent volunteers (some whom we had never seen before). The ministers came to visit and enjoyed watching the children and all the creative experiences.

Arick was sitting at the house area table with his chin resting on his arms. He began to sing the following song, "The Farmer has a penis, The Farmer has a penis, high-ho the dairy-o the Farmer has a penis."

My co-teacher ran over and sat beside Arick and said, "I think I know that song and it goes like this, 'The Farmer in the Dell, The Farmer in the Dell, high-ho the dairy-o the Farmer in the Dell.'"

Arick said, "NO!" and sang his version even louder. Michael joined him, so now we had a duet.

The chairperson of the minister's group came up to me and asked, "Shouldn't you do something about that song?"

I decided to pretend I didn't hear the song and asked, "What song?"

The chairperson, pointed to Arick and said, "That nasty song that young boy is singing!"

I then turned to the chairperson and looked him straight in the eyes and said, "I think

Arick is right, most farmers do have penises. Perhaps you would like to visit the next room to see what is going on in there."

All ten ministers ran to the next room. We did get the money, but I do not think it had anything to do with Arick's song. If I had went up to Arick and said to him, "Arick please don't sing that song, we have 'special visitors.'" Arick would have created a choir of penis singers…

Children sometimes will do anything to get attention. When they feel a sense of POWER, attention-seeking behavior begins to lessen.

Later on in this book I will discuss tips for setting up POWER SOURCES for children.

Unmet Needs

A child will do almost anything to maintain his/her role in the group, whether he/she chooses that role or was thrown into it.

Children who have unmet needs are distinguished by their regrettable ability to elicit from others the opposite of what they really need. Children who seek attention are children who need attention. The behavior may be ignored but not the need. All children come with unmet needs. Most have the ability to delay or meet these needs. Children who take us to the end of our rope often can focus on nothing else until those needs are met.

Among the most difficult situations to handle are those in which children learn to mask a feeling or need, usually behaving in a way that adults in their life only focus on their behaviors not their needs. Children don't usually know they are masking their behavior. They are simply using a method they have developed in response to having basic unmet needs.

For example, Arick would start a fight with another child rather than admitting to breaking an object that was an accident. Hitting someone else was an easy way to release feelings of anxiety or guilt.

Another example was James who really wanted to play with others, but didn't know how so he dominated most playful situations. This alienated many other children who refused to accept him in their play.

Punishment is not what these children need, although that is what they usually get. Sitting them in time-out, separating them from the group, or scolding them in public doesn't help address their unmet needs. They need to have their self-confidence built, one small step at a time, in order to kindle their feelings of trust. With support and encouragement from caring adults, they eventually will overcome their need to try to manipulate others by their behavior.

I have worked with lots of children who spent much of their time trying to take me to the end of my rope. Children who kick, push, bite, swear, break things, throw objects and do all the other behaviors often get them in trouble with adults. I've spent many hours helping children sort out their feelings and observing them to find out the causes for their behaviors. How I responded to children thirty plus years ago is not how I respond to children today. I went through many processes of relearning guidance practices that are accepting, consistent, and caring. Adults working with children waste a great deal of energy engaging in conflict with them under the disguise of discipline. Children need guidance—that is a fact. They need adults who help them develop self-respect and problem solving skills. I am hoping the next section of this book helps adults to relearn guidance practices that will lessen, rather than increase, pointless conflicts. This may require a change in basic attitudes about children. It might even require you to "GET OVER IT."

Here are the most common unmet needs I have observed:

COMMON UNMET NEEDS	
Common Unmet Need	**Reflective Behavior**
Acknowledgment	Sometimes pesters, sometimes appears lonely, sometimes appears withdraw or rebels
Communication	Talks all the time, physically acts out, distracted
Touch	Touches excessively, provokes fighting, fears touch
Socialization	Isolated, assertive, makes enemies
Encouragement	Seeks constant reassurance, avoids trying, says, "I can't"

Use this form in relearning guidance strategies for behaviors that bother you the most:

RELEARNING GUIDANCE STRATEGIES		
Behavior	**Cause**	**Strategy**
1. Whining	Attention	Ask the child, "What do you think you can do to change what you don't like?"
2. Tattling	Acknowledgement	Tell the child to say, "Tell them what you need"
3.		
4.		
5.		
6.		
7.		
8.		
9.		
10.		

PART II

Relearning Guidance Practices

"The hardest person to change is me"

Information must be Real, Relevant and hooked to an emotion.

Making Sure the Curriculum is Relevant

"What's that?"

It is normal for children to want to increase their understanding of their environment through exploration, experimentation and questioning. These kinds of experiences occur during play activities, reflecting children's needs and desires to understand the world around them. Rather than restricting their curiosity, thereby causing challenges, we should promote and encourage it. When children are given real, relevant and legitimate opportunities to satisfy their curiosity, behavioral challenges decrease.

When planning curriculum for children we must consider their social stages of play. We need to make sure the experiences we provide fit all stages of social play.

Stages of Social Play:

1. **Solitary play** – children playing all by themselves, enjoying the world through their eyes (typical of infants)
2. **Parallel play** – children playing side by side, but not recognizing each others' needs (typical of toddlers)
3. **Onlooker** – children who are watching from a distance (typical of the threes)
4. **Associative** – playing in small groups, but not recognizing rules and organization (typical of fours)
5. **Cooperative** – playing in groups, recognizing the need for each other and a willingness to cooperate (typical of fives +)

Planning experiences for children need to take into account all of these social stages. Most adults plan for the Cooperative child and forget the other social stages exist. This leads to behavioral challenges.

I observed a preschool classroom near Halloween time. The teacher sat the children in a circle and asked each of them to pay attention to the directions. The directions were:

1. A child is going to be given a plastic pumpkin, filled with treats.
2. The teacher is going to put on music, at which time, the children would begin to pass the plastic pumpkin around in the circle.
3. When the music stops whoever is holding on to the plastic pumpkin may reach inside and pick one treat.

She started the game by handing the pumpkin to Tim. When the music was started, Tim grabbed the pumpkin and held on tightly.

The teacher requested that Tim start passing the pumpkin to the music. Tim would not let the pumpkin out of his hands.

The teacher then took the pumpkin from Tim and handed it to Sue, who was sitting next to Tim. The teacher again started to play the music and asked Sue to pass the pumpkin. Sue held on with all her might.

The teacher then took the pumpkin and said the following, "Since you are not playing this game right, I will just put the pumpkin up and no one will get treats."

I could not believe what I was hearing. The children would all have to be at Cooperative play stage for them to be able to play the game the way the teacher expected. Planning for Cooperative play stage and ignoring all the others will create many behavioral issues for children.

Kenneth Horn stated, "If information provided to children is not Real, Relevant and Hooked to an emotion it will be pruned from the brain within five minutes." This explains why so much information provided to children is LOST IN SPACE. If this is difficult to believe look how often adults have made the following commands to children, "Walk," "Use your Inside Voices," "Be nice to your friends." All of which have been repeated several times during the day.

What worries me is that if children are often exposed to information that is not relevant, will their brains begin to prune automatically, without thought to whether it is important to retain or not?

In fourth grade many schools across the country ask children to memorize the states and the capitals. Many adults, when asked to recite this information, do not recall most of them. Why? Because it wasn't real, relevant and hooked to an emotion at the time it was presented. Yet at the same time if you asked adults to sing the "Mickey Mouse" song most adults know all the words, which they learned before the age of six.

So much information is being "poured" into children's brains earlier and earlier. Adults must ask, "Are we helping children to learn or prune information?"

When children are bored from experiences that are not relevant, they create their own experiences. Some of which are not what teachers want....

What is not relevant to children under the age of five?

- **The Date, Month and Year** – why is it important for them to know this information? Do they have a meeting scheduled?
- **Colors** – will the world end if they don't know their colors?
- **Shapes** – what shape is an absolute necessity for them at this age?
- **Numbers** – nowadays a calculator is all I need
- **Manners** – they need good models to practice this one

Learning for young children goes from:

- Me to You
- Simple to Complex
- Concrete to Abstract
- Home to Outside World

Making it relevant for children:

HOW TO MAKE A RELEVANT CURRICULUM

- Observe what children like doing
- Provide materials that support what they like doing
- Develop curriculum that is based on what children are interested in
- Provide lots of "hands-on" experiences
- Expand on what children already know
- Repeat experiences children enjoy
- Provide choices that are meaningful to them
- Support their learning styles
- Provide activities that focus on the process not the product
- Provide opportunities that support success
- Make it FUN

When designing a curriculum for children, especially those who take you to the end of your rope, recognize they must feel ownership in what they are doing. The child should be directing the curriculum. If you ignore his/her interest they will react by demonstrating misbehavior.

Derrick, at the easel, started to paint using the brushes that were provided in each container.

He stopped putting paint on the paper and began to paint both of his hands.

He first painted them red, then blue, etc. until he had used all the paint colors at the easel.

Denise started to walk close to him and he started to put his painted hands on her.

Denise said, "Don't put that paint on me!"

Derrick started to get closer to her.

I went up to him, got down to his eye level, and asked, "What other colors do you want to paint your hands?"

He immediately said, "Purple!"

I went to get the purple paint and asked him, "Do you want dark purple or light purple?"

In the meantime Denise wondered away.

Derrick said, "Both." I gave him both and his hands became purple…

When Derrick didn't feel in control of his experiences he often developed those that might not be acceptable. Like putting paint on Denise. When given the choice and ownership he went back to painting.

Children who take us to the end of our rope need curriculum ideas that support their interest in changing activities. Allowing these changes supports ownership.

The following are some suggestions that encourage and support changes:

Art

Children need the opportunity to stand up, use bigger brushes and become active artists. Paper size should be at least as long as their arm length. There needs to be enough space between the children who are painting so conflicts are prevented. Lots and lots of material need to be available so children are not forced to wait or share.

The larger the brush the more active they can become:

- Broom painting (sweeping paint on large sheets of paper)

- Plunger painting (using a plunger dipped in paint on large sheets of paper on the floor)

- Spray bottles (hanging large sheets of paper on a wall or a fence and fill spray bottles with diluted food coloring)

- Large paintbrushes (painting on large sheets of paper taped to a wall, or use water and buckets for pretend painting)

- Large paint rollers (moving the paint back and forth on large sheets of paper, taped to a wall)

- Mops (mopping paint on large sheets of paper on the floor)

- Large boots and shoes for feet printing (stamping their feet across large sheets of paper that have been placed on the floor)

- Snow scrapers (using large handled snow scrapers on table surfaces where paint has been placed)

- Rake painting (raking through paint on large sheets of paper)

Our responsibility is to provide an extensive variety of tools and materials so that children can experiment and become comfortable expressing themselves in positive ways.

Dramatic Play

Children who take us to the end of our rope need lots of opportunity to express their fears, anger and sadness. Dramatic play can provide these opportunities.

Make sure there are enough props so that children do not have to share. If you play grocery store, for example, and only have one cash register, you are going to have lots of "robbers," because they all want the cash register or the money in the cash register.

For dramatic play we need to think outside the traditional experiences for children. Look at the many "Helping occupations" and/or "Larger than life" occupations:

Paramedics (making sure you provide lots of bandages and stretchers)

Funeral Director (providing lots of materials for building coffins, like blocks, blankets, sheets, etc. and pretend flowers)

Hospital Personnel (providing stethoscopes, pretend needles, heart monitors, masks)

Fire Personnel (making hoses, hats, boots, ladders available)

Police Officers (providing badges, guns, handcuffs)

Forest Rangers (including logs and hoses for pretend fires, stuffed animals, binoculars)

Carwash Personnel (including large boxes for pushing cars and trucks through, tubs of water, soap, hoses, vacuum cleaners, polish)

Construction Workers (providing lots of real tools, toolboxes, goggles, lunch boxes)

Pilots (providing headsets, bottled water, chairs for passengers, lots of knobs for turning)

Race Car Drivers (providing steering wheels, goggles, helmets, gloves)

One day in my preschool classroom, I had set up the props for instigating hospital play. Jamie (a child that hit other children often) went over and started to put the stethoscope around his neck, grabbed some Band-Aids and put a mask on his face.

He started to walk around the classroom looking like he was searching for something or someone.

He came up to me and asked, "Do you know if there are any sick people around?"

I replied, "I am not sure, have you asked anyone?"

He looked at me and said, "You're not supposed to ask people if they are sick."

I said, "I didn't know that, but I'm feeling a little sick."
He immediately put the stethoscope in his ears and placed the other end on my chest.
I asked, "Do you think I will be all right?"
Jamie said, "Nope."
I asked, "What do you think is wrong with me?"
Jamie replied, "I am not sure, but I ain't going to let you die."
I replied, "I am so glad to hear that."
He began to shoot the pretend needles all over my body.
Jamie then said, "Told you I wouldn't let you die!"
Jamie for that day felt all the power in the world.

Block Play

Blocks provide not only important cognitive skills they also provide for much needed physical skills. Children need to move blocks, build them up and knock them down. Many classrooms are removing large blocks and replacing them with cardboard and/or plastic blocks.

Block play provides children the practice of using strength to carry larger and heavier blocks. Toddlers need to carry them from one area to another. Preschoolers need to lift them and stack them on top of each other. School age children need to build large enough spaces to get inside of.

One of the best prevention tools for misbehavior is the act of children using their strength in positive ways.

Adults, who work with children, are reporting everywhere, that they see children hitting and pushing more. Perhaps one of the reasons is that we are removing a positive activity like block play that enables children to use their large muscles.

The best blocks for using strength:
- Hollow blocks (some people call them window blocks)
- Large spools (electrical wiring companies use these)
- Planks of different sizes (home building stores provide free scraps)
- Large tree stumps (landscaping companies will save them for you)

Jonathon was throwing blocks in the block area. A teacher went up to him and said,

"We don't throw blocks in school, and they might hurt our friends." Jonathon threw another block and almost hit a child.

The teacher said, "Jonathon, since you can't play with the blocks the way they are suppose to be played with, you can't play with them." She directed him to leave the block area.

Jonathon left, but started to scream, "I hate you!"

Having Jonathon leave the block area doesn't help him with solving the problem. If the block play became too dangerous, then we need to help Jonathon develop an activity, with the blocks, that would not hurt other children. What if we relearn the guidance practice and include Jonathon in the process. For example, when Jonathon throws the blocks ask him, "Jonathon what can we make to catch your blocks you are throwing?" or "How can we let the other children know you want to throw the blocks?" Both include Jonathon in the decision-making and help him develop some positive strategies.

Block play is one of the types of play that adults often say causes challenging behaviors. It isn't block play that causes the challenges but how the block play is developed. Not having enough blocks, or the block building area is too small, or the types of blocks provided often are the real culprits for causing challenging behaviors. Young children often like to stack blocks on top of each other so they can run through and knock them down. This is typical behavior, especially for boys, and needs to be allowed. I always make sure that if a child is going to tumble the blocks over, that they announce it to other children around them. This often prevents children from getting hurt by any falling blocks and also gives power to the child who is knocking them over. Knocking over blocks is a good thing, and sometimes adults are going to just have to GET OVER IT!

Many adults who encounter a child, who takes you to the end of your rope, expect too much change too soon. They expect that the child will follow the curriculum and not make any changes. Children who are capable of creative misbehavior will appreciate creative and innovative responses. Children enjoy exploring curriculum that is relevant and allows for power and authority.

When you want something to change, adults must change something. Even the most experienced, successful teachers may have a difficult time allowing children the power to change what we plan for them. It is difficult to recognize that perhaps adults are the least important people in the development of curriculum. Remember, adults are only visitors to the curriculum and the children are the owners.

5 Environments That Support Children

"Whose place is this anyhow?"

I find it useful to look at an environment for children in terms of an energy system. An adult's philosophy of education is evident in the structure of this energy system. An environment produces what it presents. A clean, organized environment produces an energy system that is orderly. A disorganized environment produces an energy system that is chaos. A stimulating, creative environment is neither too clean nor too messy, but is filled with objects that produce thought and curiosity.

I imagine myself in a child's body in the space he/she will be exploring. I ask myself: "Do I feel a part of this environment or do I feel like an outsider?" "What distracts me?" "What is within my reach?" "How much space do I have to run, climb, jump?" "Does it feel good to me?"

Remember the tone and mood is set before the child arrives… This tone and mood is developed by the "invitations" we send to children through the environment that is set up. Early childhood environments should send out "invitations" that welcome children and say, "Come on in—this space belongs to you." Often children who take us to the end of our rope feel that environments do not belong to them. Therefore, they spend lots of time trying to achieve ownership. Creating environments that support their needs and interests can help them attain ownership.

The following are some elements that should be included in environments of support.

ELEMENTS IN SUPPORTIVE ENVIRONMENTS

1. Spaces for investigating – These are spaces that support children exploring, digging, taking apart, and researching.

2. Spaces of their own – These are spaces that children can call their own, no one is allowed unless invited. Examples include cubbies, shoeboxes, suitcases, and any spot that is labeled with the child's name.

3. Hiding spaces – These are spaces that children can hide from the crowds. It is important to provide opportunities for solitude. For example, sheets or blankets over tables and chairs, a large cardboard box, a loft or perhaps under a tree.

4. Climbing spaces – These are spaces where children can feel bigger than they are. For example, ladders of different sizes, step stools, stairs, and trees.

5. Digging spaces – These are spaces where children can use their large muscles. For example, sand hills, digging dams, digging for bones, digging to "China." Most sand boxes are too small for children who take us to the end of our ropes. That is why they often throw sand at each other.

6. Water spaces – These are spaces where children can handle, pour, squeeze and splash. Many early childhood programs have a water table that is often too small. Providing water in many places will eliminate the need to fight over it. For example, the house area for washing dishes, the block area for sinking and floating blocks, the art area for making mud, etc.

ELEMENTS IN SUPPORTIVE ENVIRONMENTS (cont'd)

7. Wall spaces – These are spaces that children can use for a variety of possibilities. Examples include taping up their work, hanging up photographs, looking in mirrors, etc. Many early childhood environments have walls that are too cluttered with lots of "teacher made" products. The only things that should be on the walls need to be placed there by the children.

8. Running spaces – These spaces should include opportunities for running… Children's bodies and souls say, "RUN" as fast as you can. They don't say, "SIT" often. The more children sit, the more the brain says find something more active to do. Therefore, children who take you to the end of your rope tilt their chairs, stand on the table, pound with their fists, etc. Get them up moving…

9. Loud spaces – These spaces give children an opportunity to raise their voices. If the noise bothers you then make sure the environment has area rugs or carpet. The other possibility is to buy earplugs.

10. Quiet spaces – These spaces give children an opportunity to play in a quieter atmosphere. Blocking sounds with curtains or dividers often helps. Many early childhood environments suggest that the book area or the house area is a "quiet area." Children who take you to the end of your rope do not view these areas as necessarily "quiet." We need to relearn the practice of asking children to "use their inside voice" in these areas. Not all children are capable of living up to that expectation.

11. "Herding" spaces – These spaces provide children the opportunity to play in small and large groups. Often at this age children enjoy playing "dogs" and "cats." This type of play requires space to "herd" together and hunt for food, attack when needed, make dog and cat sounds.

One day at preschool a group of boys gathered together and started to make loud "Growling" sounds. I could see that they were very excited about being a pack of "wild" dogs. Not all the children in the classroom were as excited about the "wild" dogs approaching them. So I went up to them and asked, "When is the last time you wild dogs had some food?"

They first "Growled" loudly at me and said, "We are going to kill everyone and eat them!"

My response was, "If you are really hungry, would you like to eat me plain or with some chocolate on?"

The "wild" dogs laughed and said, "We would probably like you with chocolate."

I said, "Follow me, wild dogs." They followed me toward the kitchen and I got out the basting brushes. I started to pretend to baste myself with chocolate. The activity immediately changed from "Growling" to "Basting." The children were still "wild" dogs, but just not as intimating to the other children.

If the environmental space you have "invites" children to perform in a way that is not acceptable to you than the responsibility must be yours to change the "invitation." Hallways invite children to run. If you do not want running then you have to set up the hallway in a way that gives a different message. If you have running in all areas of the environment and that disrupts other children who are playing, you have to set up the environment so that it "invites" children to run in certain locations. Adults cannot expect that children should change their behaviors when the "invitations" give the opposite messages.

If you want to decrease challenging behaviors, children must feel in control of the environment they are in. The "invitations" need to clearly send the following messages:

- You can decide where you go in this place
- You can decide how long you stay in that space
- You can change that space to make it fit your needs and interests
- You can take objects from one space to another
- You can decide what activity takes place in that space

Children cannot practice self-control until they are in environments that provide opportunities for control.

Chapter Five: Environments That Support Children 53

This might be a helpful worksheet when developing an environment for children who take you to the end of your rope.

DEVELOPING SUPPORTIVE ENVIRONMENTS	
Elements	Changes
Investigating space/s	Bury bones in sand
Space of their own	Shoeboxes
Hiding places	
A place to get higher	
Digging space/s	
Water everywhere	
Wall space clutter	
Running space/s	
Loud space/s	
Quiet space/s	
Herding space/s	

Share Soothing Skills

"Don't touch me!"

All children, especially children who take you to the end of your rope, need help with soothing skills. Learning to control anger rather than letting it control you is a very difficult awareness. It requires acknowledging signals, which occur to your body, that anger is happening. Lots of adults still do not have this skill. When children suppress tension, muscles in their bodies tighten up. Children bite their lips, grit their teeth, push outwards, yell or call names. If they do not release anger tension, it escapes on its own. You can see it when children shout, make insulting remarks, inflict pain, lash out physically or go to other extremes in order to "let off steam."

The following are a few strategies for sharing soothing skills:

Touch

Most children need to touch and want to be touched. Not all children want the same type of touch. It is important that adults observe children to find out what their comfort level is. For example, hugging is not always a soothing touch. It could be a very uncomfortable and painful touch for some children. My observation of early childhood professionals is they tend to be "feely, touchy, huggy" people. Have you ever noticed a hugger who goes up to someone who does not want to be hugged? The person they are trying to hug backs away, giving a clear signal that hugging is not what they are comfortable with, and the hugger chases them with their arms wide open. Be careful and watch for signals that children give that they are uncomfortable with certain touches. Hand holding, massage, a pat on the back, a hand on the shoulder are all good touches for some children. Boys sometimes view "roughhousing" as a positive touch. It allows them to exert their energy and touch and be touched in a way that allows for power to be demonstrated. Later on in the chapter titled "Power Builders" I will discuss "roughhousing" in more detail.

If you fear or dislike a child, your touch will immediately give you away. When you touch a child you communicate more clearly than with words. Never touch a child when you are angry, it gives a significant negative message to a child.

I like to give the thumb massage to children. When I am listening to a child and another child comes up to me and says, "Teacher, Teacher, Teacher." I take that child's hand and start to massage his hand with my thumb. I never take my ears or eyes off the child I am listening too. This gives a clear signal to the child who is requesting your attention that you are going to listen to him/her very soon, "Just Hang On."

Children carry tension somewhere in their bodies, but in some bodies the tension is more obvious than others. It is important to help children become aware of their body signals, which say they are frustrated and are beginning to lose control. This will help children learn self-intervention and/or body to mind intervention.

Examples of signals that you can help children observe in their bodies might be:

- Body temperature rising (body getting warmer)
- Hair on the back of their neck getting wet
- Hand in the air in a fist formation
- Raising their voice

Helping children become aware of these signals might prevent anger from being released in negative ways.

Asking children to sit with their bodies in a "criss cross applesauce" position or a "pretzel" position is not a posture that is physically comfortable for them. This is asking children to misbehave. Letting children select the style that is most comfortable for them reduces restlessness. When adults go to a party they are not asked to sit in a position that is uncomfortable for them.

Sucking

Sucking is a reflex that even babies, before they are born, are using to soothe their feelings of tension. So many children are being removed from breast-feeding, bottle-feeding, pacifiers, etc. before they are comfortable with the world.

The question is not, "When should the child be removed from pacifiers, etc.?" but, "What can the child use when they are fearful, or angry?" It is essential, for some children, that adults provide sucking props during stressful situations.

Some sucking props that might be provided:
- Wash cloths that are frozen and kept in the freezer until used
- Ice cubes (depending on age of child)
- Teethers that are different temperatures
- Hard candies (depending on age of child)

Some children use their shirt collar, twirl their hair, and suck on their thumb, especially during stressful situations. Adults frequently worry about some of these behaviors. Just "GET OVER IT!"

Music

For some children music is a stress releaser. You have to become a careful observer of children's responses to music. Not all children find music to be comforting. It is best to find tapes or CDs that are without words. Having music available in the background is one possibility. Remember, when you play music, children often have to get louder than the music. Another possibility is headsets for children to listen to their own selections.

Some possible CD choices are:
- *Sacred Earth Drums*
- *Gratitude, Relaxing Native American Music*
- *Misty Forest Morning*
- *The Voice of Your Heart*
- *Inner Peace*

- *Still Growing*
- *We've Been Waiting for You*
- *American Folk Songs*
- *Ocean Dreams*
- *Light Classicals*
- *Dreamland*

The rhythm of music can have a great influence on both body and mind. When you hear music with a strong beat, you may need to tap your foot or get up and dance. Music with a weaker beat generally has the opposite effect on you—you might feel like propping your feet up and relaxing. Even if children do not rest or sleep during this time, a weak beat creates a more calming effect and allows them to focus on the task that needs to be done.

Rocking

Rocking is a comfort motion that lulls the brain into deep thought. It can be in solitary fashion using a rocking chair or an adult holding a child moving forward and backwards.

The rocking motion reduces everyday stress. Some studies have suggested humble, low-tech rockers can ease the stress and anxiety brought on by high pressured, high tech lives. Some research even confirms the possibility of motion mimicking the sensation of being carried in the womb. Adult and child size rockers placed in various locations around the early childhood environment invites children to sit and regroup.

Many schools have started to place rocking chairs in school libraries, media centers, principal/director offices and they have already reported significant change for the better, especially for boys. The summary of research indicates less anxiety, disorientation, tension and even depression. It seems we need to get the children ROCKING, not a bad way to release tension.

Water

To a child water seems like the breath of life. It allows for pouring, scooping and building dams. Water beckons a child to keep exploring. Water spaces need to be available both indoors and outdoors. Indoor water tables are usually too small, and children are often expected to share the space. Instead think about using plastic wading pools on tables to create a larger space for more water or individual containers for the child who needs to be by himself/herself.

Water play should not be limited to one area in an early childhood environment, but integrated throughout the space. Running water, pouring water on your arm, shooting someone with water using a turkey baster are all forms of tension releases. The house area can have water in the sink. The block area can have a bucket of water for floating blocks. The art area can have pails of water with big brushes for pretend wall painting. All encourage children to move from high stressful situations to more calming, fun experiences.

Joey was having a hard time one morning in the preschool. Whenever a child came close to him, he pushed them down. He wasn't being intentionally mean; he was just having one of the days when everyone around him made him upset. I went up to him and handed him a bucket with some water and a large brush. He looked at me and asked, "What is this for?"

I said, "It looked like you were having a hard time keeping people away from you."

Joey said, "YEAH!"

"Perhaps you could paint a line around yourself to let them know to stay away," I said.

When a child started to get too close to him he would paint a circle around himself and say, "This means STAY OUT!" I helped remind the other children what his water line meant....

Not only was water a soother it also provided Joey with a real sense of POWER.

Stress in children stems from a number of potential causes, including family issues, developmental issues, space issues, and scheduling issues. While stress is normal, it can become overwhelming if children don't know how to handle it. Providing methods of dealing with stress gives children the tools to keep their stress under control.

Adults have a tendency to put children into "corners" when they act out from stress. Some give them a shelf in the corner-out of the way, or put them in a chair to be viewed by the other children, or have a special place called, "Time Out." These practices do not eliminate stress but often add more. We need to get children "OUT OF THE CORNERS" and into the environment. The type of environment that children live and play in affects their behavior. Factors that contribute to negative behaviors will be reduced when children are provided with environments that establish trust and sincerity. A child who is in distress often doesn't recognize the feelings of others.

 Focus On What You Want Them To Do

"I Only Remember the 'Do's' not the 'Don'ts'"

Adults can waste a great deal of energy engaging in conflicts with children under the disguise of discipline. Children need help developing skills to make wise decisions for themselves. Discipline should be geared to the development of self-respect, healthy interpersonal relationships and problem solving skills. Adults need to consider guidance practices that will lessen, rather than increase, pointless conflicts. This may require a relearning of the messages being given.

Unfortunately, many of our child-rearing methods are based on negative attitudes. Sometimes adults feel more responsible for preventing children from doing wrong than for helping the children do right. Such a negative approach fosters negative control techniques: threats, disapproval, and guilt.

Using negative statements that focus on what children cannot do only gets negative results. "We don't run in school," children might think, "You don't but I do. In fact I will show you."

If the adults say, "Walk," children often slow down immediately. The advantage of telling children what you want them to do is that they interpret the statement as "right now." Children appreciate the lack of lengthy definitions and the statement leaves the child with a positive focus.

A parent was trying to get her toddler to not go into the street. Here is the conversation that I overheard.

"Joseph, you cannot play in the street because you might get hit by a car."

"You don't want to get hit by a car do you?"

"If you are hit by a car, you will have to go to the hospital and get stitches."

"If you get stitches, you won't be able to play for a long time."

"So don't play in the streets."

What the toddler really wanted to know was, "Where do you want me to play?"

As adults we are taught early on to focus on the negative. Even when someone gives you a compliment, adults don't know how to handle it, so they turn the statement into a negative. For example, "I really like your haircut."

"Oh, didn't they do a terrible job?"

or

"That's a nice blouse."

"Oh, you mean this old thing?"

To focus on the positive adults need to relearn what they communicate to children.

When making statements that focus on what you want children to do, make sure that they can understand what you are stating or asking. Consider their individual abilities and development.

Don't expect three year olds to respond with the understanding of five year olds or that four year olds will respond with the same logic as seven years old. Keep the words as simple as possible. Say exactly what you want children to do.

Chapter Seven: Focus on What You Want Them to Do 63

The following are some examples:

FOCUSING ON POSITIVE STATEMENTS	
Not To Say	**Say**
"Stop hitting your friends"	"Did you ask them if they wanted to play that game?"
"We don't take toys away from others"	"Did you ask if they were finished?"
"What is the magic word?"	"You want this now?"
"Don't run, you might fall"	"Run over here"
"Don't call your friends names, they don't like it"	"His name is _____"
"Careful, you might fall"	"Hang on with both hands"
"Don't rock that chair"	"Rock it this way"
"People won't like you when you whine like that"	"Say it this way"
"If you keep throwing blocks you will have to leave the block area"	"Throw those blocks over here"
"You're not picking up"	"Find a place for this"
"Stop playing in your food"	"Are you finished?"
"Don't put that paint on him"	"Do you need more paper?"

64   GET OVER IT!: RELEARNING GUIDANCE PRACTICES

Helping Children Express Anger

"I'm mad and you can't make me be happy!"

When adults are asked, "What do you hope for your child?" The response typically is, "I want them to be happy." Is that the only feeling we want children to have? My hope is that children experience all feelings including anger. Children have much to be angry about. Is feeling "Happy" superior to all other feelings?

All feelings that children express need to be validated, especially anger. Feelings are responses to external events. You often don't have control over the choice of what feelings you have, but you do have a choice of what actions you decide to display that reflect those feelings.

Anger with children is usually a secondary emotion. It could mean:

- **Frustration** – they want something and are having trouble getting it
- **Disappointment** – they think something was going to happen and it doesn't
- Hurt – they feel physical, emotional or social pain
- Fear – they have anxiety about the unknown

Young children often do not know they have choices on how they respond to anger. Especially if the adult in their life is telling them to, "Come on, let me see a little smile." This implies that being angry is wrong and being happy is always the correct feeling to display.

The following are the most common causes of anger in children:

> ### COMMON CAUSES OF ANGER IN CHILDREN
>
> - Having to wait for a toy or activity
> - Having to share with another child
> - Having no space to call their own
> - Having no opportunities for power
> - Having very little encouragement
> - Having someone tell them what to do all the time

All children need opportunities to express feelings, especially anger. If they do not have opportunities to release anger they will create their own, often using other children or adults as their targets.

The following are some opportunities to release anger:

ANGER RELEASES

- Kicking and hitting boxes
- Pounding clay (not play dough)
- Tearing newspapers in strips
- Running through newspapers
- Hiding under sheets or blankets
- Hammering nails into tree stumps
- Yelling through cardboard gift wrap tubes
- Throwing paper or sponge balls
- Running indoors and outdoors
- Pushing and shoving anything with wheels
- Digging deep holes in sand
- Squirting water using turkey basters

Arick came into the classroom one morning and yelled, "No one look at me today, I am Mad!"

I turned my body so I could not see him and said, "Don't forget to let us know when we can look at you."

Arick yelled, "OK."

Some early childhood environments provide songs, and/or activities that really do not support the realistic expression of feelings. For example, the popular song, "When You're Happy and You Know It." The part that says, "When you're angry and you know it, stomp your feet" doesn't really ask children what physical action would they like to demonstrate when they are feeling anger. When I am angry I don't stomp my feet. As a matter of fact, I haven't really seen a lot of people express anger in that fashion. If you are going to use this song with children then ask them, "What do you feel like doing when you are angry?" and then display the action. Avoid making up a pretend reaction.

Another song example is, "The More We Get Together." This song implies, "The more we get together the happier we will be." I don't think so. When children are placed together with lots of other children they are expected to share, get along, be happy. So the real feeling might be, "The more we get together, the angrier I will be!"

Children's books are a really good way to help children recognize and express "real feelings." Place them around the environment in various work areas for children to look at and request to have read.

Avoid books that I call "Preachy-Teachy" that try to teach children what feelings are good and what feelings are bad. Books on manners, behaviors, etc. are not appropriate for young children. They are not cognitively at this moral stage of development. Keep the books you select for children on feelings simple, with few details, and something a child can relate to.

The following are a few examples of books that help children understand that different kinds of feelings are a good thing:

CHILDREN'S BOOKS

- *Clayboy*, Mira Ginsburg
- *Ferocious Wild Beasts*, Chris Wormell
- *The Grouchy Ladybug*, Eric Carle
- *Harriet You Drive Me Wild*, Mem Fox
- *Hungry Hen*, Richard Waring
- *I Aint Going to Paint No More*, Karen Beaumont
- *I'm Not Bobby*, Jules Phieffer
- *I'm So Mad*, Ron Miller
- *It's Mine*, L. Lionni
- *Owl Babies*, Martin Waddell
- *The Day Leo Said, "I HATE YOU!,"* Robie Harris
- *The Worrywarts*, Pamela Duncan Edwards
- *Today I Feel Silly*, Jamie Lee Curtis
- *Tough Boris*, Mem Fox
- *What are you so Grumpy About?* Tom Lichtenheld
- *When Sophie Gets Angry, Really, Really Angry*, Molly Bang

They Are Not The Terrible Twos; They Are Just Toddlers

"Watch out world, Here I come!"

Many adults who work with toddlers ask, "Why do toddlers push and hit so much?" That is an easy one. A toddler's view of the world is, "If you are in my way, I will simply move you." It is not that toddlers are mean and cruel, just very egocentric…

Toddlers are my favorite age group. They "braille" the world by touching, feeling, tasting everything. Their view of the world is truly unique to their stage of development.

A Toddler's View of the World

- "The world is a very large place. I am small, so it can be overwhelming at times."
- "I often think I am physically attached to people I care about."
- "Falling is common and it seems to bother adults more than me."
- "The changes in my mood are very sudden, often overwhelming to me. I don't know how to calm down."
- "I don't know what to do with all my energy. I hate having to sit still, when there is so much to do."
- "I don't know where my body ends and someone else's begins."
- "I don't have words to describe my feelings, so I often use my mouth or hands instead of words."

Toddlers need adults in their life that support their view of the world. Consistent caregiving with consistent routines help support the development of attachment.

Attachment is the most crucial need for all children, especially toddlers.

Remember toddlers do not have friends, they have intruders who might need to be pushed, shoved or bitten to be reminded of this.

Possessiveness is a very important skill for later social interactions. Asking children at this stage of development to share might prevent them from developing good social relationships later on.

Adults will have to relearn guidance practices with toddlers. The expectation that toddlers should know better is not realistic.

Toddlers announce with every pore of their body, "Hey World, DO YOU KNOW I EXIST?" They are not terrible, they are exciting, creative movers and shakers and adults are just going to have to "GET OVER IT!"

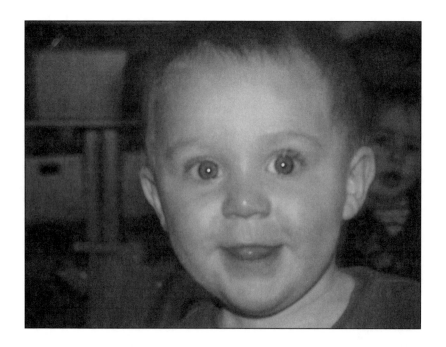

The following are some guidelines that support toddler behavior.

> ## WHAT DO TODDLERS NEED?
>
> **Social Rituals** – greetings upon entry, singing and talking during bathroom procedures, etc.
>
> **Movement** – running, jumping and climbing often
>
> **Lots of opportunity to explore** – it is the adult's responsibility to make it safe for the child to touch, move and change objects.
>
> **Ignoring "negative" behaviors** – redirect often
>
> **Distraction** – if you do not want them to throw blocks, give them soft balls, if you do not want them to climb on a table, give them something to climb on
>
> **Consistency** – in routine, in the environment and providing primary caregivers
>
> **Curriculum** – allowing children to add, change and direct experiences you provide

If adults want to have less discipline issues with toddlers the environment will need to reflect their needs and interests. Remember it is much easier for a toddler to start something new than it is for him/her to stop what they are doing.

Toddler spaces should include:

TODDLER SPACES
• Places for rolling • Places for crawling • Places for climbing • Places for banging • Places for dumping • Places for throwing • Places for poking • Places for pushing • Places for filling • Places for messing • Places for running

10 Avoid Emphasis On Sharing

"Me Sharing? I Don't Think So…"

Adults often ask me questions regarding the issue of sharing. I worry more about young children who do share than those children who do not! It is natural for young children to be "egocentric"(not recognizing that others exist). Some young children are more egocentric than others. Being egocentric doesn't mean being selfish. To be selfish you would have to recognize the needs of others, but deliberately choose not to respond in their favor.

At a preschool program, I was observing a child who pulled all the blocks off the shelf and then laid his body over the top of them, preventing any other children from playing. Many adults see this behavior and worry that he/she is not going to grow up to be a kind and generous adult. There is no evidence that documents children who do not share are more possessive as adults than children who do. Yet, there is some documentation that children who are forced to share before they are "developmentally ready" may become more possessive as they grow. Just ask first-born children.

To a young child, you never feel like giving something away until you have lots of opportunities that allow the feeling of ownership. Our job is to make sure those opportunities exist often.

Sharing is not something you teach a child, but something that is developed as he/she recognizes the needs of others. For example, if you threw a ball to a young toddler he/she will probably keep it or run away with it, thinking that is the purpose of the ball. If you throw a ball to a five year old, they are more likely to roll the ball back, knowing this is how the game is played.

The following are some helpful hints regarding sharing:

HELPFUL HINTS FOR NOT SHARING

- **Provide multiples of everything** (If you cannot provide more than one toy or object, avoid placing it in the environment)

- **Prevent battles** (By having lots of materials that are placed in smaller containers rather than one large container. For example, put clay or play dough in several small containers rather than one large piece in one container)

- **Avoid the use of timers** (They suggest outside control, rather than a personal decision made by the child)

- **Allow a child to keep an object until he/she is finished with it** (Help the child who is waiting by asking them, "What do you plan on doing while you are waiting for the truck?")

- **Encourage children to ask,** ("Are you finished with that yet?" If the response is, "No" help the child who is waiting know what their choices are while they wait)

- **Avoid praise** (For example, "I like the way you are sharing." This implies that the child who is willing to share is better than the child who chooses not too)

Let's change the rule from, "We share our toys in school" to "It is hard to share; you decide how long you want to keep it."

WHAT AGE DOES SHARING OCCUR?

- It depends on how many experiences a child has with ownership
- It depends on when a child recognizes the needs of others
- It depends on if they see an advantage in sharing
- It depends on if the child decides when and what is to be shared
- It depends on if the environment supports cooperation
- It depends on if the child wants to

There is too much emphasis on sharing. There are objects in my life that I probably will never share with anyone. I don't plan on sharing my underwear or maybe a delicious chocolate dessert or better yet, my wife. Not sharing doesn't mean that someone is less of a "good" person; it just means they don't want to share. Do you know some adults who don't have the skill of "sharing"? It takes some individuals a lot longer than others and sometimes it might never happen. You might just have to

GET OVER IT!

Avoid Mislabeling Highly Active and Highly Bored Children, Attention Deficit Hyperactive Disorder (ADHD)

"Just because I am active doesn't mean I need to be medicated"

In a Press Release from the BOSTON LIFE SCIENCES it was reported that "ADHD" is the most commonly diagnosed behavioral disorder in children. Since 1990 the total number of American children diagnosed with ADHD has risen from 900,000 to over 5.5 million, and the use of stimulant medication such as Ritalin has increased 700% in the same period. There is something seriously wrong with this picture.

The diagnosis of ADHD has become the easy way out. Many people are looking at the causes of ADHD and each year new possibilities arise. Researchers have blamed lighting, food allergies, red dye, lead content, paint colors and now chemicals used on fruit and vegetables. All which may have something to do with a few cases that were diagnosed.

My observations of classes across the country make me think there are more realistic causes of mislabeling:

- Lack of play spaces for children
- Children being inside more than outside
- Boredom
- High activity levels, especially among boys

- Teaching information that is not relevant
- Expecting children to be quiet
- Asking children to conform
- A culture that supports medication

I do believe that there are legitimate cases of ADHD, but we are also too quick to slap the label on children without first looking at changing the environment they are in.

It has been reported that the following are common observations made of young children that might get them labeled ADHD:

- Fidgets frequently
- Speaks out of turn
- Doesn't make friends easily
- Is distracted easily
- Refuses to share
- Has difficulty in taking turns

Supposedly if you have three or more of these characteristics you are more likely going to be labeled ADHD. This probably describes more than 75% of children and adults.

Seven times more boys are labeled ADHD. Higher levels of testosterone often cause a need for more physical activity. Being active doesn't mean something is wrong…

Preventing misbehavior, in most cases, is not handled by using a pill, but by changing our environment and our attitudes about highly active children. It requires adults to relearn guidance practices.

Here are some activities that support the highly active and very bored child:

ACTIVITIES THAT SUPPORT THE ACTIVE CHILD

- Stack chairs against a wall and allow children to get them as needed
- Avoid asking children to sit, "criss cross applesauce" or like a "pretzel." Let them sit the way they are most comfortable
- Expect that children will change activities that you have provided for them
- Encourage children to voice their opinion
- Accept learning style differences
- Provide for pushing, shoving, climbing and running experiences
- Introduce "relevant" experiences
- Expect children to talk more than listen
- Get children outdoors frequently in all kinds of weather
- Have fewer tables
- Make sure that most of the curriculum is "child choice"

12 Developing a Climate of Respect

"You have to give respect to receive it"

"We can't let children take something without asking. How will they learn respect?"

"We can't let children keep a toy as long as they want. How will they learn respect?"

These are the questions that many early childhood professionals ask regarding teaching children respect. Respect is not something we teach young children. It is something we model. My observations of adult and child interactions have demonstrated that most behavioral issues that involve children can be addressed when adults make changes, not when the child is forced to change.

Setting up an environment and curriculum that is appropriate for young children will create a climate that models respectful behaviors. When adults model kindness, consideration and empathy children will respond with those same characteristics.

Most concepts that are not relevant to children will be forgotten within a very short period of time. Examples include: "Don't hit your friends," "Share your toys," "Be kind to your classmates." Since these statements are not relevant, avoid using them. Adults need to change their strategies by modeling respect towards children. The results are longer lasting.

Following are some guidelines for setting up a climate of respect:

ESTABLISHING A CLIMATE OF RESPECT

- **Sharing –** Change the rule from "We share our toys in school" to "It is hard to share – you decide when you are ready." Make sure you have multiples of props.

- **Pushing/Shoving –** Make sure you ask the child that is pushing, "Did you ask ____ if they wanted to be pushed?" Then find the child something to push.

- **Taking objects –** Make sure you have the child who is doing the taking ask, "Are you finished with this yet?"

- **Fighting –** When children are involved in physical fighting, take the hands of both children and ask, "Do you both want to play this game?"(Remember fighting is often a game to young children) If they both say "YES," stay close by because there is going to be a victim soon. If one child says, "NO" have him/her say, "I don't want to play that game anymore." The adult's job is to make sure the child who wants to stop is heard loud and clear.

- **Hitting/Kicking –** Say, "I can't let you hit his arm, face, leg, etc., but I can let you hit this box." "Hit it as hard as you want too."

- **Name Calling –** Make sure the child that is being called the name says, "My name is ____, you forgot it." After the child has said this, you might have to remind the child by saying, "I heard ____ say that his/her name is____ and that is what he/she wants to be called."

Joey went up to Shannon and called her, "Hey you PIG FACE!" Shannon started to cry.

I went up to Shannon, got down to her eye level and asked, "Do you think your face looks like a PIG FACE?"

Shannon said, "NO."

"Then go tell Joey because he thinks it does."

Shannon went over and said, "I do not have a Pig's Face."

Joey looked at Shannon, surprised, and said, "Yes you do, Oink, Oink."

I went over to Joey and said, "You must not have heard Shannon, she said 'she doesn't have a Pig's Face.' Is that what you said, Shannon?"

Shannon nodded her head yes. "Joey, let's go find a book that might have a Pig's Face in it, so we can both make sure that Shannon's face is not like that."

We went over and found a book that had a Pig's Face and we both agreed that Shannon did not have a 'Pig's Face.'

When modeling respect I always have a simple rule that I follow:

Before I say or ask something of a young child I always ask myself, "**Would I say or ask that of my best friend?**"

Some examples are:

- I would never ask, "Did you flush the toilet?" in front of other adults.
- "Did you wash your hands?" before he/she sat down to eat.
- "How old are you?" in a public place.

Getting respectful behaviors from children requires adults around them to create a climate that is respectful.

13 Avoid Chaotic Transition Times

"I have a hard time waiting!"

In many early childhood settings, transition times can be a chaotic point in the day when children are getting ready and moving on to a new activity, such as snack, arrival and departures, clean up, etc. Proper planning can make a transition time easier for both the adult and child.

Children are individuals placed in a group

Remember that children are individuals that happen to be placed in a group. Limit the number of times all children have to move together in a group. Asking them to brush their teeth, attend to toileting needs, and eat all together are tasks that we typically don't ask adults to do, let alone children. The more children have to move in a group the more likely challenges will occur.

Children do not have the ability to 'wait' very long. Avoid starting the transition until you are ready for the children to move on to the next activity. 'Waiting' invites children who take us to the end of our rope to push, shove, yell, etc. to occupy their time.

Give a warning to children when there is going to be a change. I never recommend announcing to children as a group, "It is almost time to go home." Children are egocentric; they don't think you are talking to them. They sometimes look at each other wondering whom you are talking to. Go around and quietly make individual announcements. The announcement should be about what they are going to do, not what they have to do. Instead of saying, "You need to clean up it is almost time to go outside," say, "It is almost time to go outside." Children only remember what they are going to do. They have excellent 'starters,' but terrible 'stoppers.'

Avoid putting children in lines

At a preschool program I was visiting, the teacher said, "Okay boys and girls, time to get your coat on and get in line. The bus is coming."

I watched as 18 preschoolers scrambled to get their coats on and then rushed to get in line. Once they were in line a child started to push the child who was in front of him. The teacher came over and said, "We don't push our friends. You are going to have to get in the back of the line now." The child was placed at the end of the line and started to push the whole line of children. At that point the children started to scream, "Teacher, he's pushing again." The teacher came over and made the child stand next to her.

I thought to myself *How hard is it for adults to stand in lines and for preschoolers even more challenging.*

What are the skills needed to stand in line:

- Spatial (where does my body end and yours begin?)
- Time (how long do I have to stand here?)
- Recognizing Others (do they have the same needs and desires as me?)
- Self-Control (can I push when I am frustrated?)
- Delayed Gratification (do I have to wait to get what I want?)

All of these skills develop and grow at different levels and different times for each of us. Do you know some adults who do not have these skills yet?

Having young children stand in a line invites them to push and shove. It is not the child's fault but the adult who created the challenge.

Standing in line invites the child to:

- Push the child in front of him/her
- Be loud to be heard
- Knock over someone to get what he/she wants

- Run to be faster than the others
- Take it first, because he/she might not get a turn
- Do something to make sure the "world" recognizes him/her

No More Lines

- Small clusters (have children move in small clusters rather than all together at once)
- Hula Hoops (if you have to move children all together, have them hold onto a hula hoop. There is no beginning and no end)
- Hallway movements (walking is too high of an expectation; encourage hopping, slithering, crawling and running)
- Pushing activities (rather than telling children, "No Pushing," what can they push? Examples include boxes, carts on wheels, etc.)
- No waiting (prepare to move the children immediately)
- Make sure you plan for transitions (what will the children be doing if they have to wait? Examples include singing, movement, etc.)

Clean Up Time

Clean up time is one of the largest debatable transition experiences. When children are asked to clean up toys, it uses a different part of the brain than getting out toys. It is a much more complex and very difficult task. Piaget said that children have to develop "reversibility" before they are capable of reversing actions. When a child gets out a puzzle and slams it against the table upside down, it doesn't mean that he/she knows how to reverse the action. If they do not have that cognitive skill they are most likely going to leave the puzzle unfinished.

The argument for cleaning up that is often expressed by adults is that it prepares children for the future. There is no evidence that cleaning up as a young child produces adults who are better at cleaning up. In reality sometimes the opposite occurs. If clean up time is the major focus, children are not going to want to play with anything. Clean up is not the most important part of playing.

CLEAN UP TIPS

- Adults should plan on doing most of the cleaning up
- Do not expect that all children will finish playing at the same time
- Make individual warnings rather than group announcements
- Use visual warnings, especially for boys, ex. Picture cards of children picking up
- Do not expect that children will clean up the way you would
- Avoid flicking the lights; it sends children messages, especially boys, to run around fast
- Let children who want to help with the clean up process assist
- Avoid sending messages both verbally and nonverbally that children who clean up are better than children who do not

Snack Time

Snack time is another part of the schedule that sometimes invites challenging behaviors. The more choice involved in this event, the fewer behavioral challenges occur. Not all children are hungry at the same time. Providing an 'Open Snack' concept gives children the choice of when to eat and how often they should attend. The 'Open Snack' concept is where the adult provides a small table setting that invites discussion rather than chaos. Children are encouraged to be part of preparation. When 'Open Snack' is close to being finished the adult goes around the environment announcing, "If you have not had snack, now is the time." Not only are children in a smaller setting but also when they eat snack is their choice, providing lots of ownership to the process.

The need for structure is extremely important for children, especially the child who takes you to the end of your rope. For many children, the time they spend with you is the one constant in their life, the one structure they can depend upon. Children have a difficult time with constant change. It is important that you inform them of any changes in the structure of the day. Keep transitions simple, organized and few as possible.

At the snack table, David would ask me every day, "Why did the chicken cross the street?"

I answered, "I don't know."

David responded, "I don't know either." He then would laugh and laugh and laugh. He thought that was the joke. I realized quickly, since it only happened at snack time, that not only did he like to tell the joke, but also it was his way of making his routine consistent.

14 Use Encouragement Statements Rather than Praise

"You Forgot To Tell Me How Good I Am"

David was painting at an easel in a preschool classroom I was observing. He started to yell at the teacher, "Teacher look at my car I made." The teacher did not hear David and he yelled even louder, "Teacher look I made a car."

The teacher went over and responded, "What a nice car you painted. Good Job!" I don't remember David asking for an evaluation from the teacher, just acknowledgment…

Children are not born asking for praise but the underlying result from adults who give praise is a child who begins to need, crave and even depend on it for motivation and the "praise addict" is formed. A praise addict is an individual who needs consistent affirmation from others to feel confident in his or her ability or choices. Many adults use the following praise statements: "Good Job," "You're such a good boy/girl," "I'm so proud of you," "You're so smart" and many other examples. All of these statements are intended to make a child feel good. What it does is make a child depend on others for approval. They will begin to need consistent affirmation from others to feel confident in their own ability and choices. Children begin to ask parents/teachers, "Do you like my painting?" "Did I do a good job eating all my food?" and later on turn to peers for approval, which might not be what we want.

Children who take us to the end of our rope often need encouragement, not praise. They need adults who ask, "Do you need more paper?" They need adults who say, "I remember when you couldn't do that" and adults who observe, "Look how high you can kick."

> ## INSTEAD OF GIVING PRAISE
>
> - When a child asks, "Do you like my painting?" Turn it back to the child and ask him/her, "What do you like about your painting?" or ask him/her to describe what they like about their painting to other children
>
> - When a child asks, "Do you like my tower I built?" Get the child to discuss the process of making it, "How did you build your tower?"
>
> - Describe by stating the details you observed, for example, "You decided to use green paint," "You started at the top of your paper"
>
> - Focus on the process rather than the end result, for example, letter grades, "What did you to do to get that grade?" "How does getting that grade make you feel?"
>
> - Avoid evaluations of children's work, for example, "Pretty," "Smart," "Beautiful," "Good"
>
> - Acknowledge a child by stating what they have done, "Look how you are climbing up the ladder," and "I remember when you could not kick, now you can kick. Kick this box."

Observe how often you give praise; I think you will be surprised.

A child who is involved in challenging behaviors might be thinking, "I can't always live up to 'Good Job' so I won't even try" or "I will only be 'good' to get the praise." This invites children to work at getting praise rather than changing their behavior because it is the "right" thing to do.

Praise often loses its value when repeated frequently. Children begin to say, "You think everything I do is good." or "You think everyone in our school does good." If children have already achieved the praise from an adult they no longer have to move forward in their development.

Encouragement is especially important when working with children who take you to the end of your rope and seek attention and/or praise frequently. When they are given praise they often lose the skill of self-evaluation. Encouragement focuses on the process and helps the children reflect on their own work. In giving encouragement, you can help children set realistic goals for themselves based on their capacities.

In a classroom I was observing the teacher who wanted the children to get quiet in a gathering time. She started out by saying, "I'm looking for good listeners." The children continued to talk and then the teacher sang this song:

"I like the way Sara's listening,

I like the way Sara's listening.

I like the way that Sara's listening

Let's all listen like Sara."

Ralph yelled, "Sara is always like that." The teacher thought that singing this song would get the other children to be quiet and listen. What happened was that the children observed Sara's behavior as typical for Sara but not for them.

The following are some examples of praise statements that have been changed to encouragement statements:

ENCOURAGEMENT STATEMENTS	
Praise	**Encouragement**
"Good Job"	"Is there anything you want to change?"
"I like that"	"What do you like about that?"
"Nice work"	"How did you do that?"
"Good words"	"You remembered his name"
"Nice picture"	"How do you feel about what you painted?"
"Good walking feet"	"I remembered when you could not do that"
"Good choice"	"You have decided to _____"
"Beautiful"	"Look at all the colors you used"
"I like your smile"	"Does this make you happy?"

15 Providing "Real" Choices

"Don't offer a choice unless you plan on accepting my response"

When we give children choices we give them opportunities to be in control of their lives. All individuals need to feel in control of portions of their life. The more opportunities we give children to make decisions the greater the feeling of personal freedom.

"Real" choices are those that children will be able to clearly decide on and offer positive alternatives. "Do you want to sit at circle time and listen to this story?" or "Do you want to sit by yourself and listen to the story?" is an example where the child doesn't have a choice on whether or not he/she really wants to listen to a story at all.

"Real" Choices

- ✓ Do I have to come to circle/gathering time? (Are children required to attend circle/gathering time if they are really involved in something that is more important to them?) I think the most successful gathering time would be one where children never showed up....

- ✓ Do I have to sit down to eat? (Can children have the choice of standing up to eat?) Sitting down is not necessarily good for the digestive system.

- ✓ Do I have to pick up toys by myself? (If children are required to pick up toys can they have an adult who helps or does most of it?) Remembering that picking up is not the most important part of play…

- ✓ Do I have to always listen to what you say? (Children only collect what is important to them, so lots of information is pruned if it is not relevant)
- ✓ Do I have to do what you tell me to do? (Children who take us to the end of our rope are looking for avenues to gain power and/or control) If they frequently have to do what they are told, they don't feel in control of their lives.

Adults need to look how often during the day is child-choice vs. adult choice. The more activities that are chosen by the adult the more challenging behaviors occur. When you stop to analyze it, you may be amazed to realize that you have literally been telling children what to do without very little room for decision-making by them.

If you have children in your program who have had very little opportunity for making choices you might have to start out with fewer choices and then increase the complexity as they become comfortable.

Adults frequently fall into the trap of thinking they are allowing children to make choices when, in fact, they themselves are making the decisions. Adults want to avoid giving choices to children and than taking their response and ignoring it. For example, "Do you want to get your pajamas on? It is time for bed." The child might respond with, "Thanks but I am going to stay up and watch David Lettermen." The adult then responds with, "I said get your pajamas on." That is not the original choice…

Another example I have observed in many early childhood programs is when a male child is holding onto his penis and jumping up and down (the universal sign that he needs to go to the bathroom), the adult asks, "Do you have to go to the bathroom?" When a child is given this choice and has to choose between 'playing' or 'going to the bathroom' they frequently choose 'playing.' The child responds with, "No." The adult then says, "You better get in there before you wet your pants." Again, it's a choice that was given and then taken away.

Never give a choice that is not a choice. When adults end a sentence with "okay?" it says to the child there is a choice in the matter. Sometimes the word "okay" is added to a sentence unconsciously. Some examples of this are:

"Time to wash your hands, okay?" or "Don't forget to throw your napkin in the waste basket when you are finished, okay?" or "It is time to get ready to go home, okay?" All suggest a choice, but in reality there isn't.

When listening to children and giving them "real" choices, you can help add to their feelings of self-worth and their desire for control/power.

When my daughter was about three years of age, she was going to attend a cooperative nursery school program for the first time and I was going to be the participating parent. It was in January, very cold and lots of snow. On the morning she was to attend I opened the closet door and asked my daughter, "Jennifer, what would you like to wear on your first day of nursery school?"

She glanced at all the clothing and picked out her "Wonder Women Swimming Suit."

Here I was, an early childhood specialist, giving my daughter a choice that she gladly took. I said to Jennifer, "That is a good choice for home, how about we wear this one or this one?"(I showed her some clothing that would probably be better for the weather).

Her response was, "No! I want to wear my Wonder Women Swimming Suit." Well because I believe that once you give a choice you must follow through with the response, my daughter (three years of age) and I (a six foot tall early childhood specialist) started off walking towards her nursery school. I did not give her the choice about wearing a coat, hat and boots over the swimming suit. We arrived at the nursery school and because it was the first day many parents were standing around talking to each other.

When I arrived I said to Jennifer, "You might want to keep your coat on; it is rather chilly in here." At that point Jennifer unzipped her coat and opened it wide so everyone could see that wonderful choice, the Wonder Women Swimming Suit. All of the parents took one look and their mouths opened wide in surprise. I turned to them and said, "What can I say, she likes Wonder Women!" and told Jennifer, "Have a lot of fun today" as I left the building. Did my daughter become ill, or was her day ruined because of her choice? I don't think so. I did learn a very important lesson. Do not give a choice if you are not ready to accept the response…

16 Support Risk Taking

"I can do it!"

Can you remember the things you did as a child? If you are like most adults you will probably remember:

- Freedom of play without a lot of supervision
- Playing with children who were different ages and perhaps you didn't know them
- Using material that was found rather than bought
- Sorting out conflicts yourself
- Making your own judgments about risk

The potentially risky things you played might have included climbing trees, playing near water, riding fast down hills, climbing boulders and perhaps building forts, castle, etc.

My observations of children, especially those that take us to the end of our rope, are much less likely to be exposed to risk taking and learning about risk. Last year, almost three times as many children were admitted to the hospital after falling out of bed as those who had fallen from a tree.

What are the benefits of risk-taking?

- ➢ Increases the resilience of children
- ➢ Helps them develop problem solving skills
- ➢ Creates safer playing
- ➢ Helps them make better judgments

All of these benefits are skills we want children to obtain. Adults have a responsibility to ensure that they offer children all these opportunities.

Everyday life always involves a degree of risk and children need to learn how to cope with this. If we observe children from an early age, they are motivated to take risks—they want to learn to walk, climb, ride a tricycle and are not put off by the spills and tumbles they experience as they attempt to build coordination and control.

Children who are sheltered from risk taking when they are young will often not be able to make judgments about their own capabilities and will not be well equipped to resist peer pressure in their later years. Children who learn in their early years to make their own reasoned decisions, rather than simply doing what they are told to by others, will be in a stronger position to resist the pressures they might face as they reach their teenage years.

What kinds of risk taking opportunities do children need?

- Physical risks (learning how to negotiate natural hazards, physical environment and developing coordination of their bodies)
- Social risks (understanding expectations of rules, developing reasoning skills and learning to negotiate with others)
- Intellectual risks (trying out new ideas, solving problems, and being inventive)

Some children enter our programs without much opportunity or awareness of risk-taking. These children might need some 'gentle' shadowing. Children cannot be responsible for their safety. That must be the responsibility of the adults. Adults must be responsible for equipment placement, maintenance and repair and removal when necessary.

Some risk taking possibilities might include:

RISK TAKING POSSIBILITIES

- Children building "higher than their eyes"
- Children climbing on large boulders
- Children climbing on ladders
- Children going Up the slide, rather than Down
- Children crossing on planks of wood over water
- Children jumping from a climber or platform
- Children standing up on swings
- Children using ropes
- Children sliding down a pole
- Children throwing balls
- Children painting blindfolded
- Children using real tools like hammers, saws
- Children digging with real shovels
- Children drawing with branches in the sand
- Children standing on a chair
- Children rocking a chair
- Children hiding under a table

Dr. Sandseter, a professor of psychology at Queen Maud University in Norway identified five categories of risky play:

- High speed
- Handling dangerous tools
- Being near water or fire
- Rough and tumble play
- Wandering alone away from adult supervision

There is no evidence that playground safety measures have lowered the average risk on playgrounds. Actually in some cases it has been reported that some injuries, like fractures of the arm, increased after the introduction of softer surfaces on playgrounds.

Learning to cope with risk and to accept challenges is a vital part of human development and learning. Those who have been denied this learning might not have the resources to cope with and retain control of their lives. Children who take us to the end of our rope need help to develop competence. This competence can be developed as they experience trusting their own responsibility through risk-taking.

How many of you remember climbing up the slide, even though your parent or teacher said not to? All the way to the top and yelling down, "I am the king of the castle, you're the dirty rascal!" and you are still alive to talk about it.

17 Fighting?

"No Hitting, Are You Kidding Me?"

Children learn to use physical force by seeing others use it and by having it used on them. They do not generally want to hurt others. When young children use physical force, it is purely an emotional reaction and usually done without thought and without malice. When we place children in a group it is natural to expect fighting to occur. Saying, "No Hitting" is too high of an expectation. They happen to be individuals who have been placed in a group. Many children who take us to the end of our rope have very little social skills yet are asked to function in a group setting without pushing, shoving or hitting.

Adults working with children often confuse the terms 'assertive behavior' and 'aggressive behavior.' It is common for adults to ask me, "How can I handle this aggressive child?" When I have a discussion with them, I find out usually the child they are talking about is not aggressive but an assertive child.

Aggressive children plan on hurting or destroying someone or something. You can often hear it in their communication. For example, "I am going to hurt you" or "I am going to break this apart." In both of these examples, the child is planning and following through with his/her actions. This type of behavior often requires one-on-one guidance and frequently the child cannot remain in a group setting.

Assertive children are looking to get recognized or acknowledged or are seeking independence. They will say, "I am first down the slide" and push the child away or "I want the bicycle first" as they knock over other children to get to the bike. It isn't planned, and often is an emotional response to a need they have. This type of behavior requires redirection, changes in the environment or in some cases just GETTING OVER IT.

Most children that I have observed with behavioral issues are assertive, not aggressive. They often push, shove and grab to have their needs fulfilled. It is normal and should be expected.

Children fight over the most mundane reasons. The most common types of fighting:

- Issue Fighting ("My dad is better than your dad." "You cannot play with me, because you don't know how.")

- Possession Fighting ("I had this truck first." "This is my clay and you can't play with it.")

- Attention Fighting ("Get out of my way." "Move away from me.")

In most cases fighting is often annoying squabbles and adult intervention delays the process of children working it out themselves. This is assuming that there is no true harm, physical or emotional infliction being done. In that case intervention is a must.

Many adults fall into the trap of trying to investigate who started the fight, and why it started. Taking sides or finding the bully is not the crucial issues in regards to fighting. The goal is to remove the "winning" and/or "losing" out of the challenge.

When children use physical forms of fighting, adults need to observe children to see if intervention is required. Preventing physical forms of fighting means creating an environment that promotes self-control. An environment needs to provide children with choices to be made where they can be in control of their decisions. Saying to a child, "We don't fight in our school, it might hurt our friends" doesn't say to a child what they can do when they are mad, frustrated or eager to gain attention.

Dameon said, "Jack is so stupid."

I asked, "What does Jack do that makes him stupid?"

Dameon said, "He stands too close to me all the time!"

I said, "You don't like it when he stands that close?"

Dameon said, "Yes!"

I said, "Let's show Jack how close you want him to you."

Dameon said, "OK!"

RELEARNING GUIDANCE PRACTICES FOR FIGHTING

Issue Fighting

Child Said	Restate
"My dad is better than your dad."	"You really like your dad."
"You can't play with me, because you don't know how."	"You want him/her to play the way you want?"
"My picture is a lot better than yours."	"You really like your picture?"
"You aren't playing that game right."	"Show him/her how you would like them to play."

Possession Fighting

Child Said	Restate
"I had this truck first."	"You are not done with the truck?"
"This is my clay."	"You don't want to share the clay?"
"You can't play with the blocks, they are mine."	"You decide how many blocks you want him/her to have."
"He is my friend, not yours."	"You want him to only play with you?"

Attention Fighting

Child Said	Restate
"Get out of my way."	"Where do you want him/her to stand?"
"Move away from me."	"How far do you want him/her to move?"
"You're stupid."	"He/she isn't doing it the way you want?"
"You poop face."	"I don't see any poop on his/her face."

If intervention is required the following steps are recommended

1. Take hold of the hands of the children fighting
2. Ask, "Do you both want to play this game?"
3. If they both say yes, step back and watch closely, because there is going to be a victim soon
4. When you notice there is a victim, step in and ask, "Do you still both want to play this game?"
5. If one of the children says no, then say, "You need to say, 'STOP!'"
6. Have the child who wants to stop say, "STOP!" loudly
7. You repeat what the child says, "I hear him/her say she wants to 'STOP'"

If fighting occurs and a child is being hurt, the following steps should be taken

1. Firmly take the child's hand who is hitting
2. Ask the child who is being hit, "Do you want his hand in your face?" (Be specific, state where the child is hitting)
3. Ask the child who is being hit to say loudly, "Stop hitting my face!"
4. Adult supports by saying, "I heard ____ say he/she doesn't want you to hit their face."
5. Give the child who is hitting something they can hit (box, pillow, hammer and nails, etc.)
6. Say to the hitter, "Since you want to hit, hit this hard." "This you can hit a lot."

Children need many opportunities to learn to work out problems among themselves. It's important for adults to distinguish between behavior that calls for immediate intervention and behavior that is just part of normal developmental exploration of control. Making such a distinction can greatly reduce the number of times you need to assume the role of police officer.

18 Preventing Power Struggles

"You can't make me; you're not my mom!"

How often have you heard the above statement said by a child? Sometimes when a child makes this statement you might even be thinking silently, *I am so glad that I am not your mother.*

A power struggle is an individual need for control and/or power. All species are looking to gain power. Sometimes a child will do anything to attain power/control. Even if that means creating "hurt" or "chaos." Have you notice that when a young child is playing a game of "Candy Land" and they think they are going to lose, they will say, "I don't want to play anymore." When my brother, who is one year younger than me, and I played Monopoly and he thought he was going to lose, he would "accidentally" knock over all the hotels on the board. It is not easy losing power. Clare Cherry said, "Children cannot be successful at losing until they have lots of opportunities to win."

When do Power Struggles most likely occur?

- Mealtimes
- Clean up time
- Nap time
- Group time
- When sharing is requested
- Arrival and departures
- Sometimes all the time

Notice the basic similarity in all of these is that the times are directed and/or decided by the adult. My experience with young children show that the more the child is in control of their schedule, the fewer power struggles. We need to look at our daily routines and see how much of the day is "Teacher Decided" versus "Child Decided."

Children who wish to attain power are looking for a variety of ways to achieve it. PUSHING BUTTONS is a very attractive and easy way for children to immediately receive power. They are looking for adults whose buttons are easily pushed. It is important that adults make the choice not to let challenging behaviors be a constant "button pusher." For example, the child who comes up to you and pokes your arm, all the while saying, "Teacher, Teacher, Teacher." Or the child who puts their arms across their chest and says, "I'm not going to pick up and you can't make me!" As soon as the adult starts thinking privately, "I'll make you, you little _____," they have hooked you. Every time the child produces that kind of attitude he/she has pushed another "button." The feeling of power continues to fulfill their needs. Adults have to ask themselves:

- Do I have any control over it?
- Can I do anything about it?
- Is it really that bad?
- Will the world end if I don't say or do something?

If you can't answer yes to all of these, GET OVER IT!

My observations of classrooms demonstrate that the more opportunities that exist in the child's environment to attain power, the fewer power struggles occur.

I observed from a distance the following. Charles was at the top of the climber saying loudly, "No one can come up here, and I mean it!" Of course that did not set with children who also wanted to be at the top of the climber.

Craig yelled, "You're not the owner of this!"
Charles then responded with, "I am not the owner, I'm the BOSS!"
Craig paused and then asked, "When can I be the Boss?"
Charles without hesitation responded with, "When I am done."
Craig then asked, "How long?"
Charles asked, "You want to be a Boss too?"
Craig immediately responded, "Yes."
Charles said, "Come on up, but I am the first Boss."
Craig said, "Okay" and up he went.

Here is a partial list of what I call POWER BUILDERS.

POWER BUILDERS

- **Moveable parts** – Suitcases that can be carried around (avoid the ones on wheels). Crates with and without wheels. Nets and bags for capturing "wild beasts." Wagons, Wheel barrels.

- **Large Construction** – Lots of room for pounding, sawing, sand plasting (Black and Decker has a small size, perfect for children)

- **Climbing** – Ladders, rope nets, hills, chairs, wood boxes, going up slides

- **Digging** – Lots of sand, real shovels (hardware stores have great metal shovels with round edges that are used for smaller gardens)

- **Being LOUD** – Yelling in plastic tubes or piping, getting inside large boxes and creating echoes

- **Spontaneous Singing** – Letting children sing songs they have made up at all parts of the day

- **Steering Wheels** – Find steering wheels at "junk" car dealers. Children pretend to be race car drivers

So many times children can solve their own Power Issues if adults avoid stepping in too early… Children cannot develop Power unless we give them opportunities to practice self-control. Remember to ask yourself before assisting, "Will the World End, if I don't step in?"

19 Bring Back Roughhousing

"It's Not World Wide Wrestling"

Do you remember playing Red Rover, Red Rover? Did you play it this way? "I'm coming but I'll be gentle," I don't think so. Matter of fact, you probably took a running start and smashed into the line of children holding hands, trying with your whole body to break the chain and bringing lots of children down with you.

There are many fears and misconceptions surrounding roughhousing. One of the biggest fears is that roughhousing may cause violent behavior later on in a child's life. For young children, especially boys, roughhousing is universal and is often craved. There is no research that indicates that playing roughhousing, as a young child, increases the chances of violent behavior as an adult. Matter of fact just the opposite seems to occur. Roughhousing has considerable merit in a young child's development according to Anthony Pellegrini. Through the physical interactions that take place during roughhousing, children learn the give-and-take of appropriate social interactions. This give-and-take mimics successful social conversations and interactions. The social roles practiced and learned in roughhousing provide children with the social knowledge needed for future relationships.

Roughhousing is not "world wide wrestling." Children are willing participants who join the play readily and eagerly and remain as long as the play sustains. In "wrestling" one participant is usually dominating another one. The focus is on winning, not playing....

To support roughhousing it is important that adults provide a safe environment. It cannot be the child's responsibility to make sure his/her play experience is a safe one.

The following are some tips for making safe areas for roughhousing:
- Hard edges need to be rounded
- Rugs need to be skid free
- Enough space is needed to move around
- Surfaces need to absorb the shock of falling
- Areas need to be away from the direct line of traffic

The adult's role in supervising roughhousing is to assist children in recognizing body language or body codes. For example, when two children are roughhousing and one child raises his/her hand in a fist formation, the adult's role is to tell the child what he/she may do with their hand (for example, " grab his leg" or "take your hand and put it around his arm"). When a child looks fearful or frustrated the adult might say, "Are you finished playing this game? You can tell him to stop."

Often getting children to learn respect is a concern of adults working with children. Supervising roughhousing provides for opportunities to model avenues of respect. When a child takes something that belongs to someone else, the adult can ask, "Did you ask first?" When a child is anxious about being hit, the adult can ask, "Do you want his hand in your face?" When a child looks like they are finished playing the game, the adult can ask, "Do you want to continue playing this game?" When a child is doing something to another child that is not acceptable, the adult can ask, "What would you like him/her to do?"

This type of modeling adds words, which the child can use, to control his/her play experiences.

Roughhousing is not a center or area of the environment. It is spontaneously occurring play. It takes place both indoors and outdoors with adult guidance and supervision. In my experience, supporting roughhousing often sees a decline in challenging behaviors.

Do you remember as a young child having an adult in your life that would get down on all fours, which invited you to jump on his/her back and play "horsey" or an adult who grabbed your head by wrapping their arms around you and giving you the "knuckles"? You would scream, "stop that" but then would try to do it to them…. I am hoping you will bring roughhousing back.

The following are some activities that support roughhousing.

ACTIVITIES THAT SUPPORT ROUGHHOUSING

- Red Rover, Red Rover
- Ring Around the Rosie (their favorite part is "all fall down")
- London Bridge (favorite part "Lock them up")
- Motor Boat, Motor Boat (start out slow and move to fast)
- Kick the Can (start with small tin cans and move to larger ones)
- Billy Goat Gruff (acting out the story)
- Arm Wrestling (don't forget to lose)
- Tag (chasing games are fun)
- Tug of War (large rope)
- Sword fighting (swimming noodles)

20 Supporting Super Hero Play

"I'm Faster Than a Speeding Bullet"

I have not always been in favor of super hero play. In my earlier years as a teacher, super hero play represented a violent portrayal of society's influence on young children. Now, I am a "born again" super hero supporter. What happened? I began to read Vivian Paley's work on why children play super hero play. In her worked titled *Superheroes in the Doll Corner* (1984), she states "Luke Skywalker and Darth Vader have the same domination as Mothers and Princesses. When boys play Darth Vader it involves lots of conflict and action. When girls play mothers and princesses it involves lots of pesty characters that have tantrums, sister quarrels, babies crying and mothers threatening and spanking."

What is super hero play? It is a form of creative or pretend play in which children imitate action heroes that they admire. In a child's social and moral development, playing 'good guys' versus 'bad guys' is very normal and important for their growth.

If you don't let children play super hero play or gunplay, what will you replace this type of play with that is just as powerful…?

Both boys and girls play super hero play. The difference often is that boys tend to be more physical in their responses. Girls tend to be more verbal in their responses. Both boys and girls require the same responsiveness from their teachers.

Jacob, wearing a cape, was in the sand area throwing sand in the air. He was yelling, "Watch out for my magic dust, it will turn you into monsters."

Sara was close to Jacob, wearing her usual cape, and yelled, "Stop throwing that magic dust around, it is making my eyes water."

What does Super hero play offer young children?

- **The power to dominate** – All children want and need to dominate in their play. Sometimes that means giving orders, taking objects, and giving directions.

- **The power to make solutions** – Developing self-control requires children to develop a variety of solutions.

- **The power to gain control over 'fears'** – Young children have many fears, including but not limited to ghosts, goblins, witches; someone breaking into their room at night; the world disappearing when the lights go out; clowns and other physical changes. Being a super hero allows them to practice gaining some control over these fears.

- **The power to develop language** – Children who often choose not to use verbal language often create "power" words to increase their vocabulary. "May the Power Be With You," "I am going to 'Zap' you," and "Let's sword fight" all are examples of this 'power' language.

- **The power to use lots of physical energy** – Young children, especially boys, need lots of opportunities to use physical force. Letting them practice pushing, shoving, climbing, jumping, etc. helps them with this important need.

- **The power to begin to recognize the differences between "good" and "evil"** – These concepts are very difficult for young children. Super hero play gives children the opportunity to experience both sides (saving the world from mass destruction, or becoming the evil villain).

The more opportunities we give children to attain power, the fewer children will need to create negative behaviors. Every species, no matter what age, is looking for power.

The adult's role in super hero play is extremely important to its success.

- Avoid turning super hero play into a moral issue. Keep it developmental. "Remember not to hurt your friends, it isn't nice" is an example of a statement that moves super hero play into a moral issue. A statement that keeps the play at a developmental level is, "Ask him if he wants to play that game."

- Make sure that the children playing super hero play want to play. The adult needs to make sure that there are no victims in this play. When you see an anguished face ask, "Do you want to play this game? You can say NO."

- Make sure the space is safe and large enough to play super hero play. Children cannot be responsible for playing safely. The adults might need to move some tables or cabinets, add a mat, etc.

- Have parent/guardian meetings that discuss TV and video viewing habits. What children are watching, how often and with whom are all-important subjects. I am not a believer that boycotting television viewing is the answer. I do believe that sitting with children and discussing what children are watching and limiting the amount and type of viewing is.

- Provide props that enhance children's super hero play. For example, capes, swords and ropes. They should be part of the regular dress up props. Types of swords can include swimming noodles (cut to size), newspaper (rolled and taped), and paper tubes (gift wrap cardboard tubes).

- Stop any hurtful language. Ask the child who is being called a name, "Do you want to be called that? What would you like to be called?"

- Give children alternatives over fearful situations. Providing props for fire fighting, capturing wild animals, emergency care play or chasing games. In these types of play the "evil" is not always a person.

Zero Tolerance Policies have been developed in programs all over the country within the last ten years. These policies often exclude lots of opportunity for children to attain power and control. Roughhousing, super hero and gunplay have almost been eliminated in many programs. Reviewing the research claims, the zero tolerance policies have not decreased aggressive behavior; in fact, they have increased in some areas. What the policies do not take into consideration is how children can attain their need for POWER.

120   Get Over It!: Relearning Guidance Practices

Every species, no matter what age, is looking for POWER!

21 Creating a Place to Belong

"Whose Place Is This Anyhow?"

After completing a keynote on children and violence a conferee asked me, "Are children more violent today than they were 20 years ago?" I am not sure that children are more "violent" but what children are exposed to that relates to violence has increased. The research indicates that children do not have to be directly involved in violence to feel the effects.

I think there are three changes that have occurred that impact children directly.

1. **The lack of Safe Havens** – those surroundings that were considered safe for children were schools, places of worship and home. In the last five years many incidences of violence have occurred at these sites.

2. **Family affirmations** – this involves learning of respect, creating positive expectations and a feeling of belonging. In our hurried times these opportunities sometimes do not exist.

3. **Positive communications** – listening, sharing of feelings and expression of frustration. Who can children go to for sincere active listening?

Everyone is looking for a place to feel a sense of "belonging." Children who take us to the end of our rope especially need a climate that says, "You are important and need to be here."

Arick started out in my program not trusting me, the other adults and children. He displayed lots of behavior that he thought would make him feel a part of us. He shoved, pushed, hit and name called—all in the name of wanting to be recognized as a crucial part of his new place. It took the adults in the classroom to relearn practices that helped him feel a sense of belonging.

"Everyone is looking for a cave"

WHAT IS NEEDED TO CREATE THAT ENVIRONMENT OF "BELONGING"

✓ **Create Safe Havens**
- Provide for consistent routines/schedules (take few field trips and avoid parties)
- Provide for both individual and group spaces (make sure children have a chance to be alone)
- Provide positive "invitations" (greet children with enthusiasm and honesty)

✓ **Create Affirmations**
- Acknowledgement – not praise – for positive behaviors (you like to hit, let me show you where you can hit)
- Celebrate differences (make sure we notice differences as a positive opportunity)
- Create feelings of belonging (the climate should support trust)

✓ **Create Positive Guidance Practices**
- Use a preventive approach (look at your environment and make changes that prevent challenges)
- Include the community in the process (include the community in your playground, parent meetings, etc.)
- Model the problem solving approach (help children recognize the real issues)

✓ **Create playful experiences**
- Provide opportunities for children to attain POWER (letting children make real choices)
- Support dramatic play and/or pretend play (encourage play that allows children to express all feelings)
- Provide lots of opportunity for active games (helping children to be able to control their bodies)

Conclusion:
Do I Really Have to Change?

"When you want something to change, you must change something," Leo Tobin. I believe that 98% of challenging behaviors are due to either the environment, the curriculum or the adult practices. So guess who has to change? Change is not easy; it requires relearning.

Discipline techniques must be more than just devising strategies to make children do what we want them to do. We can do that. We have all the rewards and consequences and techniques. But do they meet the child's needs? Do they treat the child with dignity? A child who takes us to the end of our rope will answer these questions for you. You will know quickly and clearly whether you have met a need or only managed a behavior temporarily.

To make changes you must:

- Realize that it is all right for children to express anger. Where and how is the adult's responsibility.

- Realize that discipline of children is more about establishing relationships of trust.

- Realize you can prevent many problems by being positive, clear in your expectations, flexible and caring.

- Realize you must offer "real choices" for children. Not choices that are often taken away once the child makes the choice.

- Realize we must establish good habits of communication, giving acknowledgement not praise, offering encouragement and clarifying messages.

- Realize you sometimes just have to "GET OVER IT!" by ignoring small annoyances, not turning developmental behaviors into moral responsibilities.

I hope this book has provided you a journey into the behaviors and needs of the child who take us to the end of our rope and to enhance your understanding of the child's total needs. Children are empowered when given daily opportunities to demonstrate who they have become, what they have already created in their lives, and what they want their lives to be.

If you have a child that takes you to The End of Your Rope, sometimes you need to increase the length.

Additional Resources

Bilmes, J. *Beyond Behavior Management*

Bos, B. Chapman, J. *Tumbling Over the Edge*

Brown, S. Play: *How it Shapes the Brain, Opens the Imagination and Invigorates the Soul*

Carlson, F. *Big Body Play*

Cherry, C. *Please Don't Sit on the Kids*

Chairk, J. *Time In: When Time Out Doesn't Work*

Elkind, D. *The Hurried Child*

Elkind, D. *Miseducation*

Garbarino, J. *Lost Boys*

Gartrell, D. *Guidance Approach for Encouraging Classrooms*

Hodgins, D. *Boys: Changing the Classroom, Not the Child*

Jensen, E. *Teaching with the Brain in Mind*

Johnson J. & Denita D. *Let Them Play*

Jones, G. *Killing Monsters: Why Children Need Fantasy, Super Heroes and Make Believe Violence*

Kohn, A. *Punished by Rewards*

Kostelnik, M.J., Whiren, A.P., Soderman A. K., Stein L. & Gregaory L. *Guiding Children's Social Development*

Letts, N. *Creating A Caring Environment*

Louv, R. *Last Child in the Woods*

Oehlberg, B. *Making it Better*

Paley, V. *A Child's Work: The Importance of Fantasy Play*

Paige, N. *Taking Back Childhood*

Reynolds, E. *Guiding Young Children*

Rice, J. A. *The Kindness Classroom*

Shumaker, H. *It's OK NOT to Share*

Smith, C. A. *The Peaceful Classroom*

Tobin, L. *What Do You Do With A Child Like This?*